SWANSEA
This was your life!

By David Roberts

First published in Great Britain in 2010
by Bryngold Books Ltd.,
100 Brynau Wood, Cimla,
Neath, South Wales SA11 3YQ.

www.bryngoldbooks.com

Typesetting, layout,
editing and design
by Bryngold Books

Copyright © David Roberts 2010

All rights reserved. No part of this publication may be reproduced, stored in a retrieval system, or transmitted in any form, or by any means, electronic, mechanical, photocopying, recording, or otherwise without the prior permission, in writing, of the copyright holder, nor be otherwise circulated in any form or binding or cover other than that in which it is published and without a similar condition being imposed on the subsequent publisher.

ISBN 978-1-905900-19-0

**Printed and bound
in Wales by
Gomer Press,
Llandysul, Ceredigion.**

Contents

Appreciation	4
Foreword	5
A never ending story	6
Street scene	7
Familiar faces	43
District days	57
The performers	73
Guiding lights	83
Parties & parades	97
School report	111
Moving along	127
Taking a break	141
Working ways	151
Mumbles & Gower	163
Sports view	173

Appreciation

I am once again indebted to so many people for their help and encouragement in the production of **Swansea - This was your life!** My thanks in particular are due to the Lord Mayor of Swansea, Councillor Richard Lewis, for contributing his kind foreword. The book would not have been possible without the support of people from far and wide who have shared their pictures from the past. These include:
Roy Kneath, Ray & Dorothy Lewis, Geinor & Peter Tremewan, Geoff Rees, the late Betty Key, Robert Wayne Davies, Barry Griffiths, Hugh Rees, Julie Jones, Blanche Hurn, Phyllis Thomas, Steve Phillips, Alan Lloyd, Ashley Lovering, Barbara Griffiths, John Jones, Bernard Humphries, Christine Rix, Rev Roy Bevan, Clive Cockings, David and Eluned Govier, Colin Andrew, David Lile, Dennis Spinks, Dilys Frayne-Timothy, Dolores Ramos-Morgan, EJ Trick, Eileen Jenkins, Gay Davies, Gaye Mortali, Gaynor Emery, the late Dennis Scanes, Gloria Wilson, Grahame Michael-James, Haydn Davies, Hilary Evans, JV Hughes, Jim Davies, Jodie Jones, Julia Bennett, Julie Cole, June Shakeshaft, Kathryn Owens, Keith Roberts, Alan Williams, Malcolm Williams, Marilyn Evans, Michael Jones, Gloria Rees, A Williams, Bert Barton, GM James, WA Bevan, A Jones, Delma Mainwaring, T Fossey, Noel Blows, Norman Sullivan, Pamela Parkhill, Peter Johns, William Bateman, Robin Wayne, Rodger Green, Roger Evans, Roger Trollope, Royston Morgan, Russ Thomas, Christine Thomas, Steve Davies, Sandra Walters, Steve & Sandra McCulloch, TB Harris, Terry & Joy Osborn, Trevor Davies, WG Humphreys and James Ackland.
Others without whose help the book would not have appeared include Gerald Gabb, David Beynon, John & Barbara Southard, Anthony Isaac and Neil Melbourne.
Finally, no one will be more surprised than me that this is my 25th book on the Swansea Bay area. There is one person without whom I could not have completed one, let alone that number. It is of course my wife, Cheryl. To her more than anyone I say thank you for your never-ending support.

Share your pictures

You too, can play a part in recording the history of your area by contributing photographs to the next Swansea nostalgia book. Please telephone 01639 643961 or e-mail david.roberts@bryngoldbooks.com to discover the ways in which you can do this. We would be delighted to hear from you. All photographs, transparencies, negatives, black and white or colour, of people, places, events, streets, buildings, schooldays and sport are considered whatever their age, subject or format. They are all promptly returned. Also, if you have missed any of the previous 12 books then contact us now as some titles are still available.
You can also check out our web site at
www.bryngoldbooks.com
for details of our other fascinating local nostalgia books.

Foreword

Like the many books from David Roberts before it, *Swansea – This was your life!* reflects much that has occurred in the city down the years.

Despite having already gathered many thousands of images into what has evolved as a fantastic, ever-growing album, David still continues to amaze us by unearthing and sharing fresh photographs from the past. Each of these plays a part in preserving memories of our Swansea as it was and our forbears too as they went about their daily lives, at work, rest and play.

Swansea – This was your life! offers us a unique comparison of today's city against the way it once was and allows us to judge how change has slowly manifested itself. What started as just one book for David, has now become 13 in consecutive years. This is something that few towns and cities across the length and breadth, not only of Wales, but the whole of Britain can boast. This new title and its predecessors serve as a unique, easily accessible, people's archive.

The book can be compared to a cake where each of the chapters, from street scenes to sport and school groups to transport is a deliciously tasty slice of all our past lives. Many aspects of our community are featured. Standing out this year is a special section dedicated to 100 years of Guiding in the area. Once again it shows how changes have taken place in this commendable movement.

My own memory serves to remind me of how things were and how much has changed, but there are lots of occasions when a glance at a photograph like the many in this book is enough to revive long-forgotten thoughts of people and places that were once familiar.

David has once again done much to capture the spirit of the past. We applaud him for this and hope his efforts will continue long into the future.

Swansea – This was your life! is something of which the city can be proud.

Councillor Richard Lewis
Lord Mayor of the City & County of Swansea
September, 2010.

A never ending story

The word 'new' has heralded many changes throughout Swansea in the past decade. The arrival of new homes, new shops, new commercial enterprises, new roads and even the new people they often bring with them, have all played a part in what has become an almost seamless metamorphosis into modernity.

Sometimes these changes have been minimal and insignificant, but often they take on a far bigger role. The growth of the sprawling SA1 docklands development and its impact on the main eastern traffic gateway to Swansea is a prime example. There are others that could be reeled off, from the city's rapidly emerging new bus station to seafront apartment blocks and the central shopping development. They change the skyline and they change our lives.

Many will consider these changes a healthy sign. They are after all a demonstration that Wales' unbeatable seaside city is keeping pace with the fast moving 21st Century. Others however, will lament the fact that to make way for the new, much of the old has first to be brushed aside.

These differing opinions are an indication of the continual conflict that is bound to exist as the city reshapes itself to meet modern demands. Both sides of course, feel justified in their thinking and their sentiment.

Both sides though will surely be united in their desire to maintain Swansea as a vibrant and prosperous place, something that cannot be achieved without change.

Much of the change experienced down the years, decades and even centuries in the city is mirrored on the pages of Swansea - This was your life! The title is perhaps apt as many of the images contained within them are moments in time encapsulated forever.

Added together the images in this book will unite generations and perhaps spark an enthusiasm for finding out more about what all the modern day newness has replaced. Switch on the television, turn the pages of our local newspaper and what is happening right here, right now will be evident. Turn the pages of this book however and what will be revealed is much of what has paved the way for these developments in the never ending story that is Swansea.

David Roberts,
September, 2010.

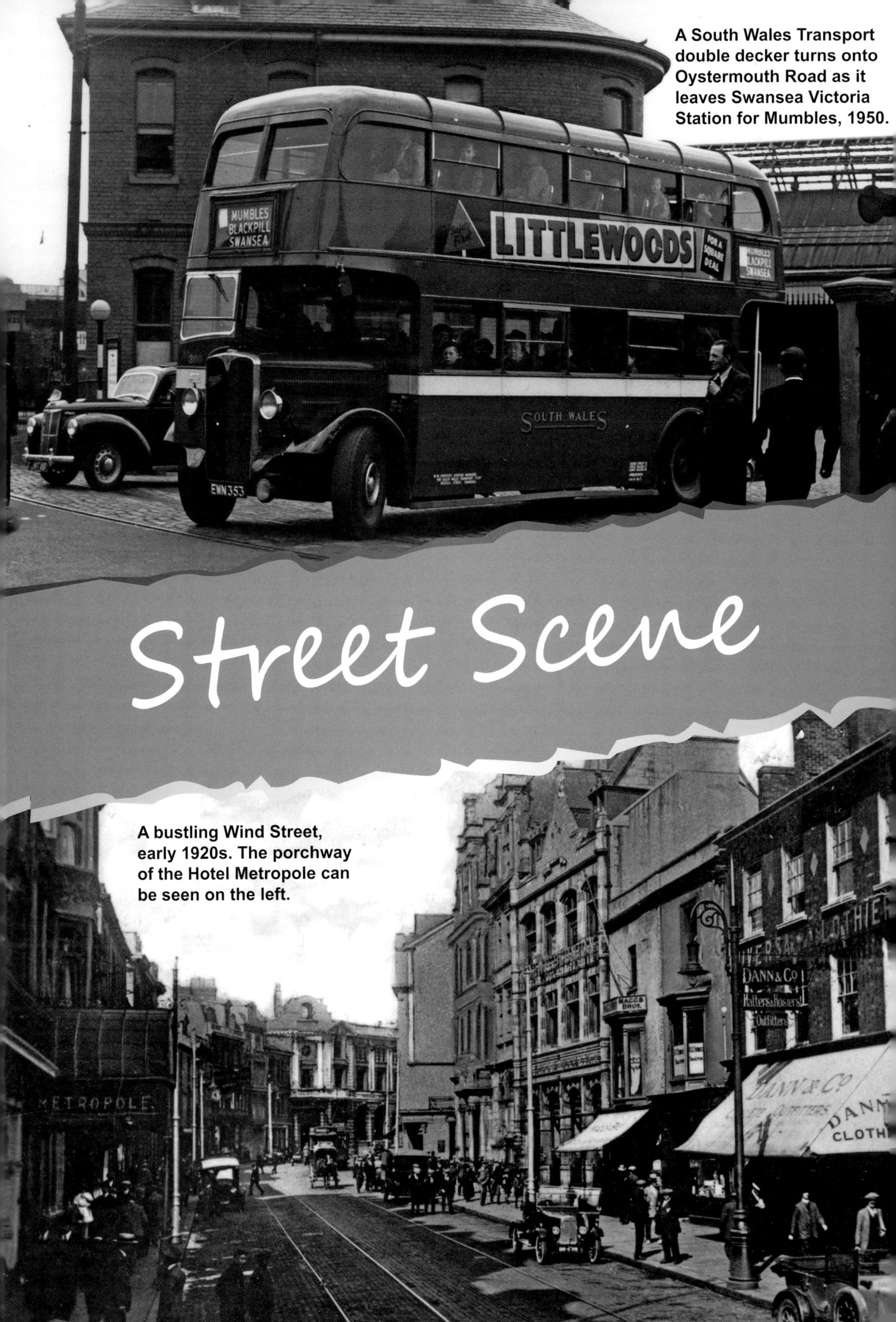

A South Wales Transport double decker turns onto Oystermouth Road as it leaves Swansea Victoria Station for Mumbles, 1950.

Street Scene

A bustling Wind Street, early 1920s. The porchway of the Hotel Metropole can be seen on the left.

The statue of Sir Henry Hussey Vivian commands a fine presence in Castle Square, in 1903. This location is better known today as Wind Street. The statue has long since been relocated to St David's Square. The impressive building on the left is the Ben Evans department store which failed to survive the ravages of wartime bombing in 1941.

The White Rose family and commercial hotel, Walter Road, 1903. Perhaps one of the men standing outside is its proprietor, Mr D Jones.

Worcester Place which stretched from the Castle towards Welcome Lane, early 1900s.

Looking eastwards along a busy Oxford Street with the Market, and its impressive main entrance on the right, 1903.

Ivy Place and the forecourt of High Street railway station, mid-1930s. The Grand Hotel is on the right and St Thomas just visible in the distance.

The Royal Cambrian Institution for the deaf and dumb, The Graig, Mount Pleasant, 1903.

Dillwyn Street at its junction with Oxford Street, mid-1950s. The buildings with arched frontages are temporary shops erected following Swansea's wartime bombing. The junction with St Helen's Road and the Kingsway is in the distance and the roof of the YMCA building is just visible.

Traffic squeezes over the River Tawe swing bridge, early 1950s. Today this vehicular gateway to the city is served by a much larger road bridge as well as a second crossing up river.

Part of the vast Weaver's Flour Mill complex. The overhead passageway led to the cake mill, early 1950s.

STREET SCENE

Looking across College Street towards Woolworth's and other shops in High Street early 1950s. Woolworth's was severely damaged in the wartime blitz and the top floors had still to be repaired.

Castle Bailey Street, looking towards Castle Street, mid-1950s. Castle Gardens, on the left, had replaced the blitzed Ben Evans department store.

SWANSEA – THIS WAS YOUR LIFE!

The special Suit Week in the C&A fashion store, Portland Street, may have been the attraction for these two night-time window shoppers, 1965.

A view across central Swansea towards Castle Street, during early post war rebuilding. The framework of the David Evans department store is under construction, 1952.

STREET SCENE

These pigeons were having a hard time finding a drink in the frozen water of the fountain that for many years was the centrepiece of Castle Gardens, 1977.

A mixture of TV aerials make an interesting skyline silhouette in this Swansea east-side street during August, 1967.

Oystermouth Road showing the gas works, August 1966. The Tesco Marina supermarket is there now.

SWANSEA – THIS WAS YOUR LIFE!

The steel skeleton of the Dragon Hotel rises skywards in this view across the Kingsway roundabout, from Princess Way, 1960.

A panorama of Swansea Docks and the mouth of the River Tawe, taken from Kilvey Hill, 1969. Mumbles Head and lighthouse can be seen in the distance.

STREET SCENE

Maritime-themed decorations adorned the Victoria Park elevation of the now removed Slip Bridge in 1966.

SWANSEA – THIS WAS YOUR LIFE!

Weaver's grain store and, on the right, the Cuba Hotel, 1960.

Buildings at the lower end of The Strand, 1972. The bridge carried a high level railway line from East Dock and High Street station to the South Dock.

Swansea's head Post Office, Wind Street, 1967. It was opened in 1901.

Vehicles wait at the traffic lights near the former main entrance to Swansea Docks after the opening of the new River Tawe bridge, 1972. The arches on the left once carried railway traffic at high level to and from the South Dock.

21

Under construction at the time, the Griffith John Street residential tower block commands the eye in this panorama of the late 1960s.

Oxford Street School, viewed from Dillwyn Street, early 1960s. After its demolition it became a short stay car park.

Terraced properties along Oystermouth Road, mid-1970s. Most appear to be empty, perhaps awaiting demolition.

STREET SCENE

Looking along Oystermouth Road, with its guest houses, towards The Slip bridge, 1974. The filling station on the right, beside the Trafalgar pub, is advertising petrol at just 68p a gallon!

Looking along Western Street, past the Singleton Hotel and into Singleton Street, 1976. The BT tower is visible in the distance.

SWANSEA – THIS WAS YOUR LIFE!

Looking along Singleton Street, with the Grand Theatre on the far right, 1976.

A view across Swansea centre towards the mouth of the River Tawe showing the Vetch Field, still with its West Stand, mid-1980s. Alongside is Swansea prison.

STREET SCENE

Low tide in the River Tawe before construction of the barrage, 1979.

Looking over the rooftops of properties in Wind Street, including the old Post Office, from the top of the BT tower, May, 1984.

Castle Gardens in its full glory as a city centre haven, mid-1980s. The Caer Street building, top left, was formerly named Beau Nash House and home to gents outfitters Sidney Heath.

Castle Square, the replacement for the green haven that was Castle Gardens, 2000. Many who loved the gardens complained that the concrete expanse was drab and uninspiring.

STREET SCENE

A view of the Guildhall across the floral clock and gardens at Victoria Park, 1982. The clock told not only the time, but that this was also the Year of the Castle.

Looking westwards along the Kingsway into St Helen's Road, 1985.

Construction underway on Sainsbury's supermarket and the adjacent Homebase DIY store alongside the River Tawe, February 28, 1985. Swansea Docks is visible across the river.

An atmospheric peep through Salubrious Passage into Wind Street, on a wet evening, 1985.

SWANSEA – THIS WAS YOUR LIFE!

Swansea Harbour Trust offices viewed from the top of the BT tower, February 28, 1985. This is now the home of Morgan's Hotel.

Swansea Maritime and Industrial Museum with some of its waterborne exhibits moored alongside pleasure craft in the South Dock marina, 1989. The leisure centre and BT tower are on the left.

STREET SCENE

The Quadrant shopping centre can clearly be seen in this panorama. Behind it the skeletons of three gasometers that were soon to be replaced by a Tesco supermarket and car park. In the distance, rows of apartments now line the sea shore, July 26, 1989.

Looking up High Street, from its junction with College Street, towards the station, November 1989. The towering office block in the centre is Alexandra House.

SWANSEA – THIS WAS YOUR LIFE!

Demolition underway on Jimmy Wilde's guest house, Alexandra Road, near its junction with High Street, June 1986.

STREET SCENE

The promenade on the seaward side of the South Dock marina looking towards the Pump House restaurant, on the far left, 1985.

The clock on the side of the former Boots the Chemist store, Princess Way, 1992.

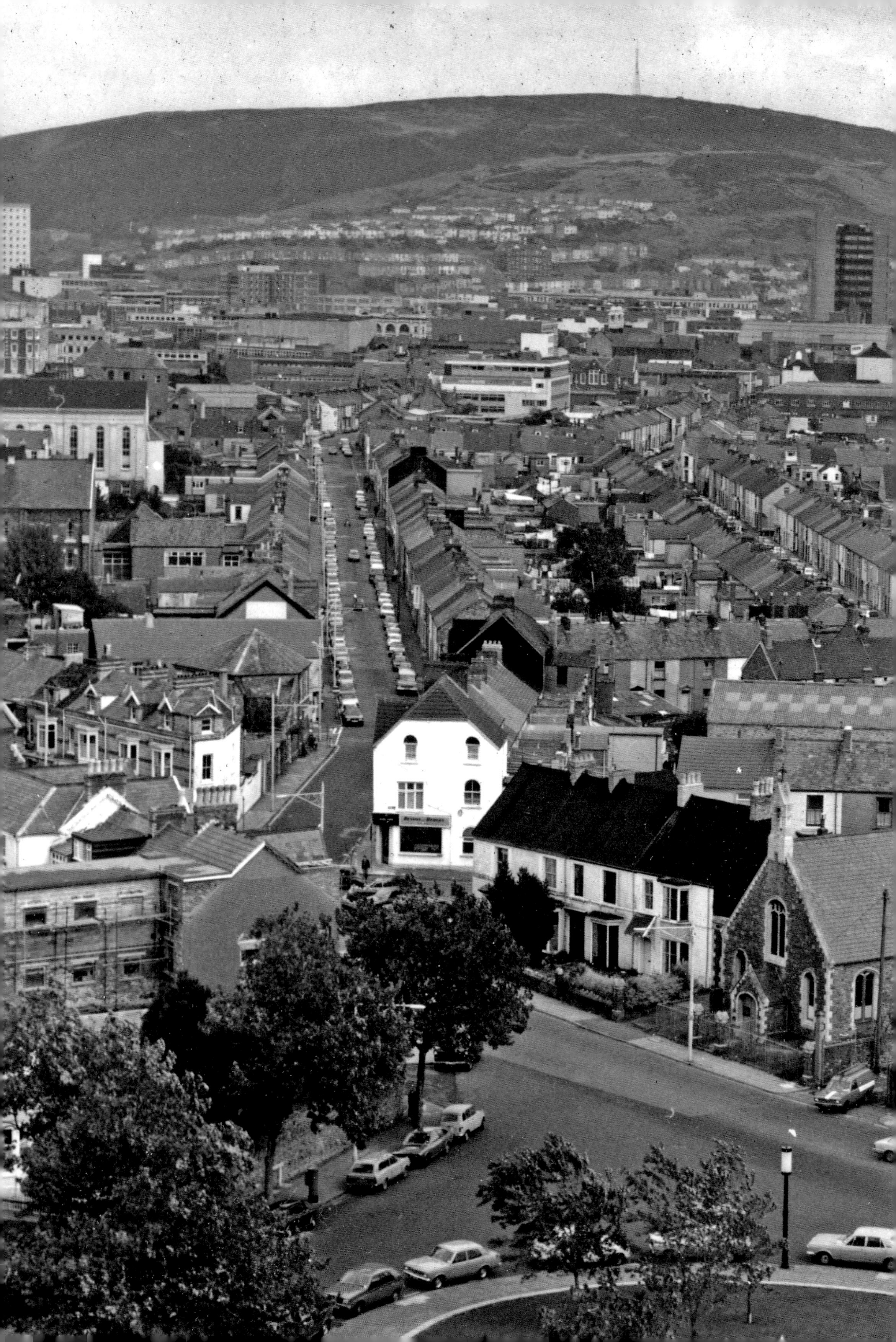

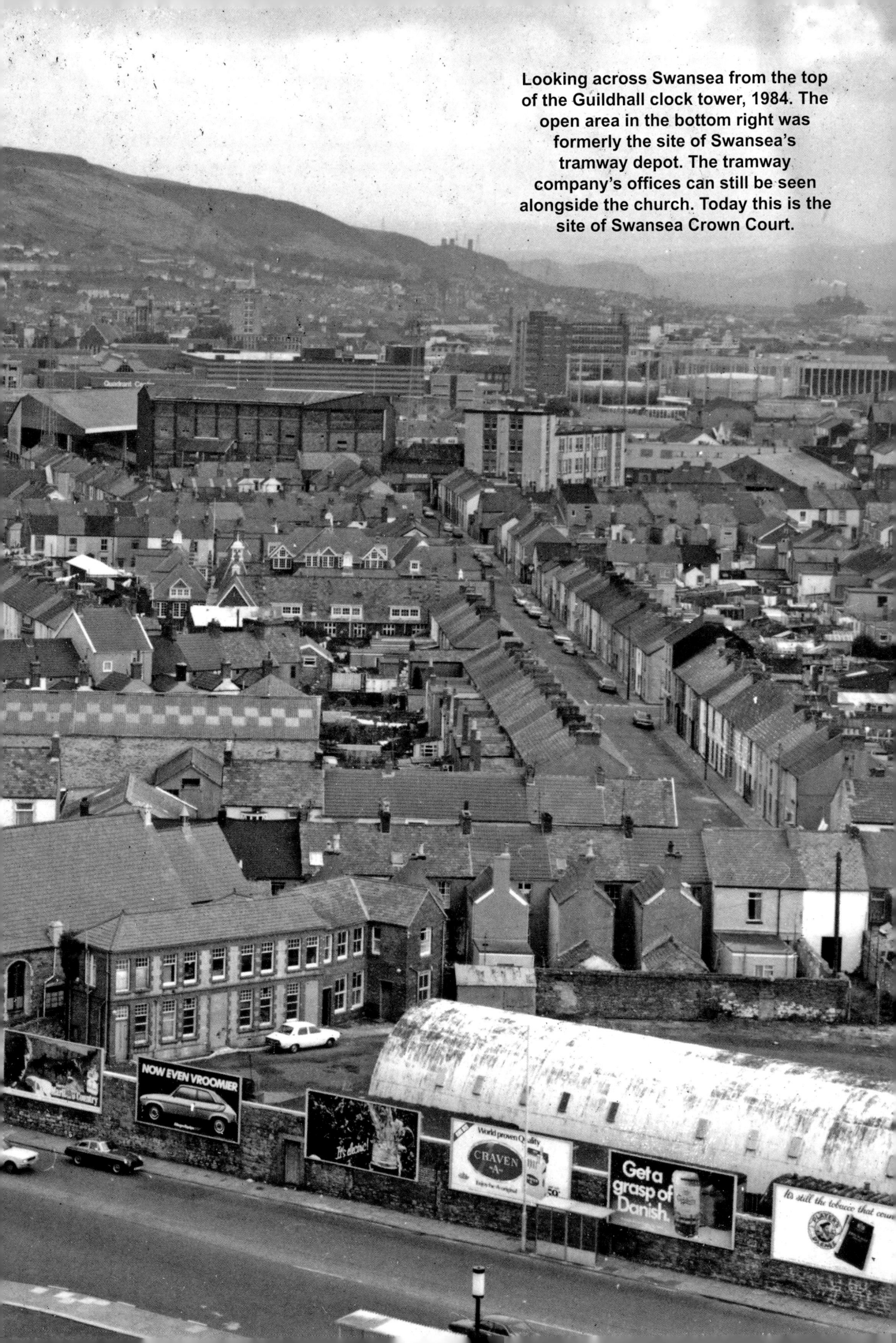

Looking across Swansea from the top of the Guildhall clock tower, 1984. The open area in the bottom right was formerly the site of Swansea's tramway depot. The tramway company's offices can still be seen alongside the church. Today this is the site of Swansea Crown Court.

SWANSEA – THIS WAS YOUR LIFE!

Swansea Crown Court, St Helen's Road, shortly before completion, 1987.

Oystermouth Road, between County Hall and Swansea Prison after heavy overnight snow, 1991.

STREET SCENE

The remains of Swansea Grammar School, Mount Pleasant, November, 1995.

The BT tower overshadows Swansea Castle during upgrade work to clad the outside with reflective glass, early 1990s.

SWANSEA – THIS WAS YOUR LIFE!

The familiar grandstand on the sea side of Swansea rugby and cricket club's St Helens ground presents a lonely spectacle on the day work began on its demolition, August 22, 2005. The scene below was what greeted passers-by just a day later.

STREET SCENE

Swansea YMCA at the junction of Page Street and St Helen's Road, June 1995.

Demolition work underway on the David Evans store, Princess Way, March 9, 2007.

SWANSEA – THIS WAS YOUR LIFE!

Refurbishment work underway on the Patti Pavilion, November 11, 2007.

Work begins on raising the Meridian Tower apartment block and restaurant alongside the South Dock marina, November 11, 2007.

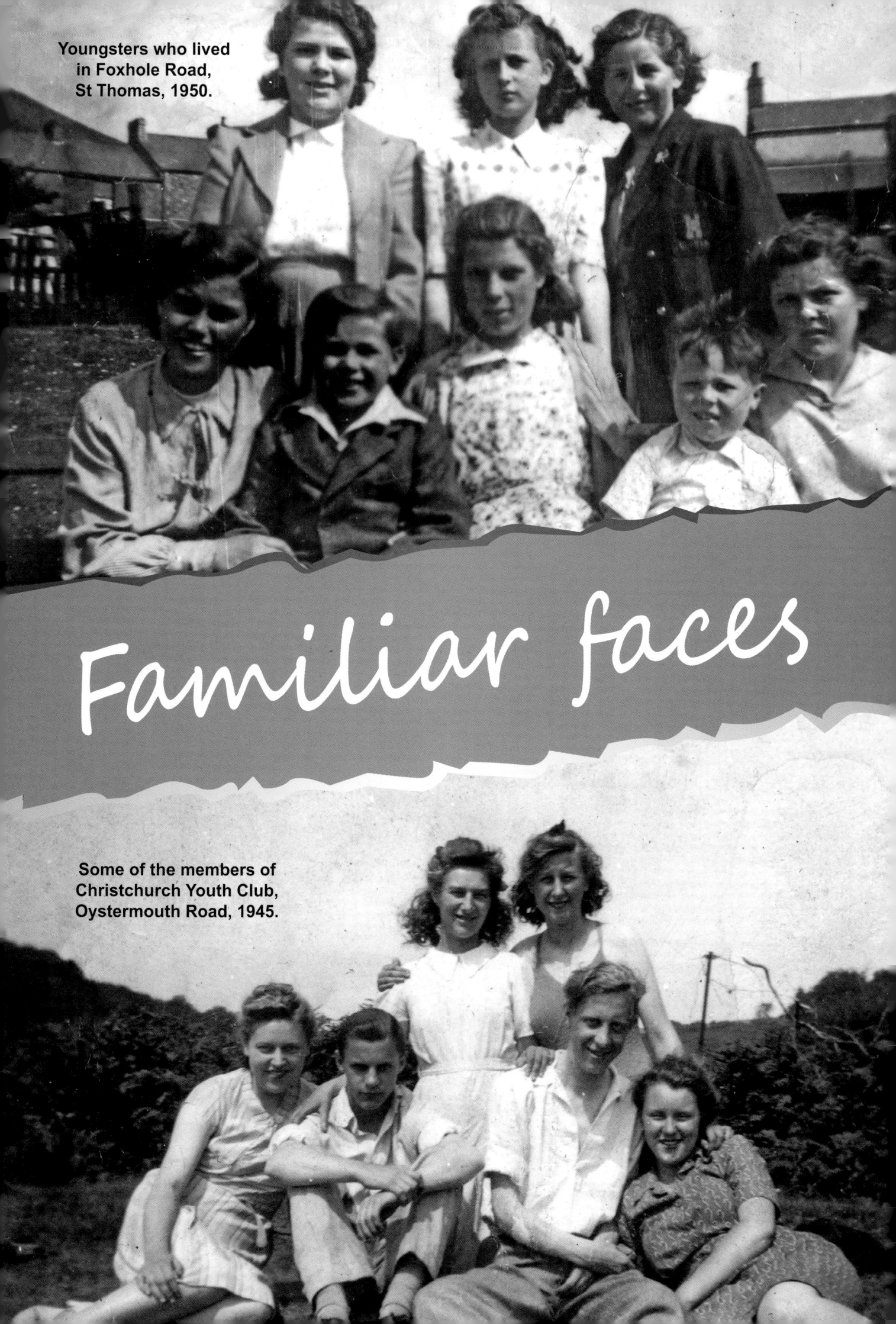

Youngsters who lived in Foxhole Road, St Thomas, 1950.

Familiar faces

Some of the members of Christchurch Youth Club, Oystermouth Road, 1945.

SWANSEA – THIS WAS YOUR LIFE!

Members of the youth club which met at the back of Church House, St Helen's Road, a hostel for clergymen, 1944.

One for the album — taken after the wedding of Ronnie Fisher, of Manselton, and his bride Doris Richards, of Treboeth 1948.

FAMILIAR FACES

A group of friends opposite St Thomas Church with St Leger Crescent behind them, early 1950s.

Members of Hafod Brotherhood, early 1950s.

Members of Mount Pleasant Band of Hope, 1954.

Young men in Miss Cascarini's cafe, St Thomas, in the early 1950s. She was the sister of Joe Cascarini of ice cream fame and her cafe was a long-time popular rendezvous.

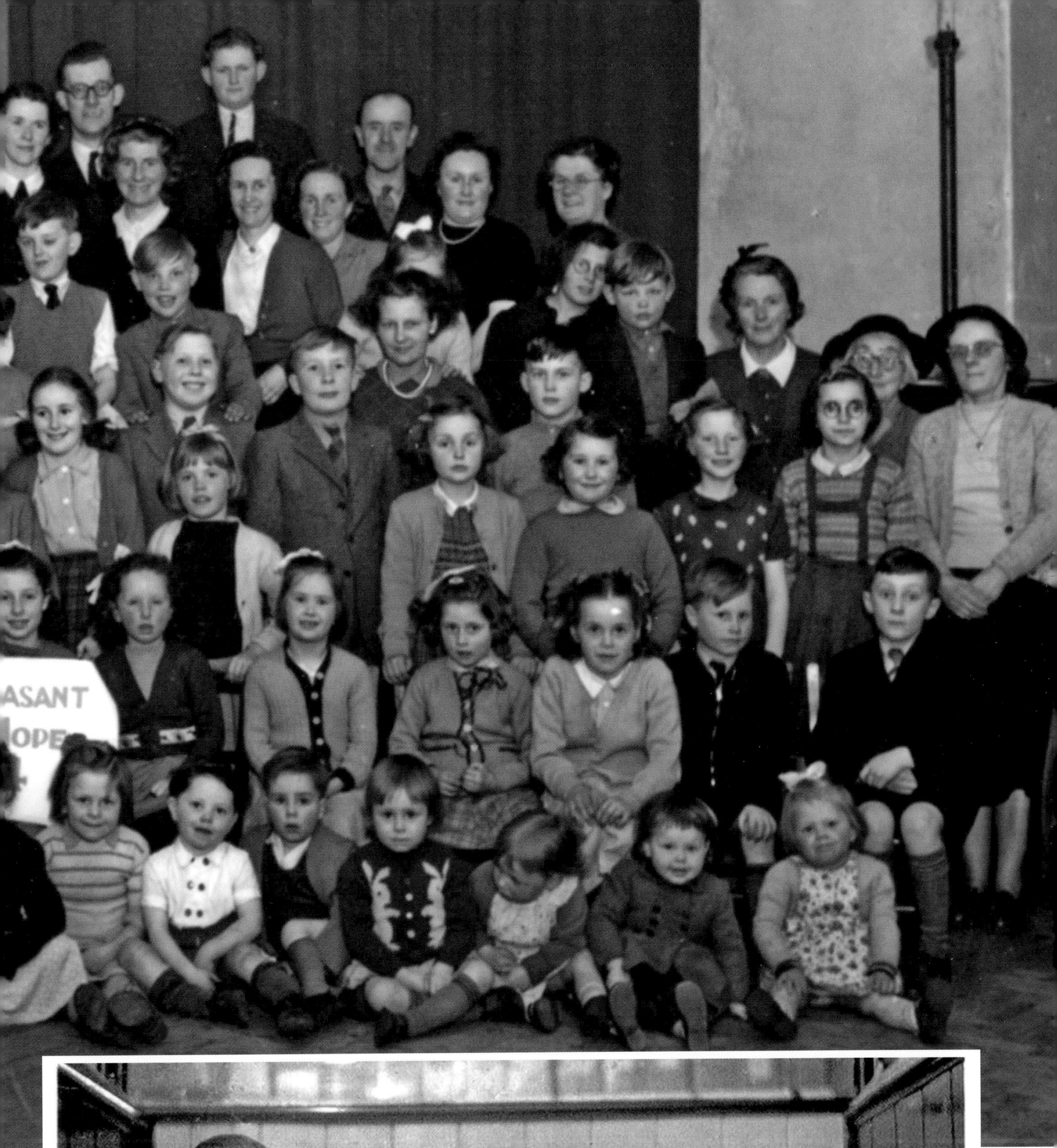
ASANT
OPE

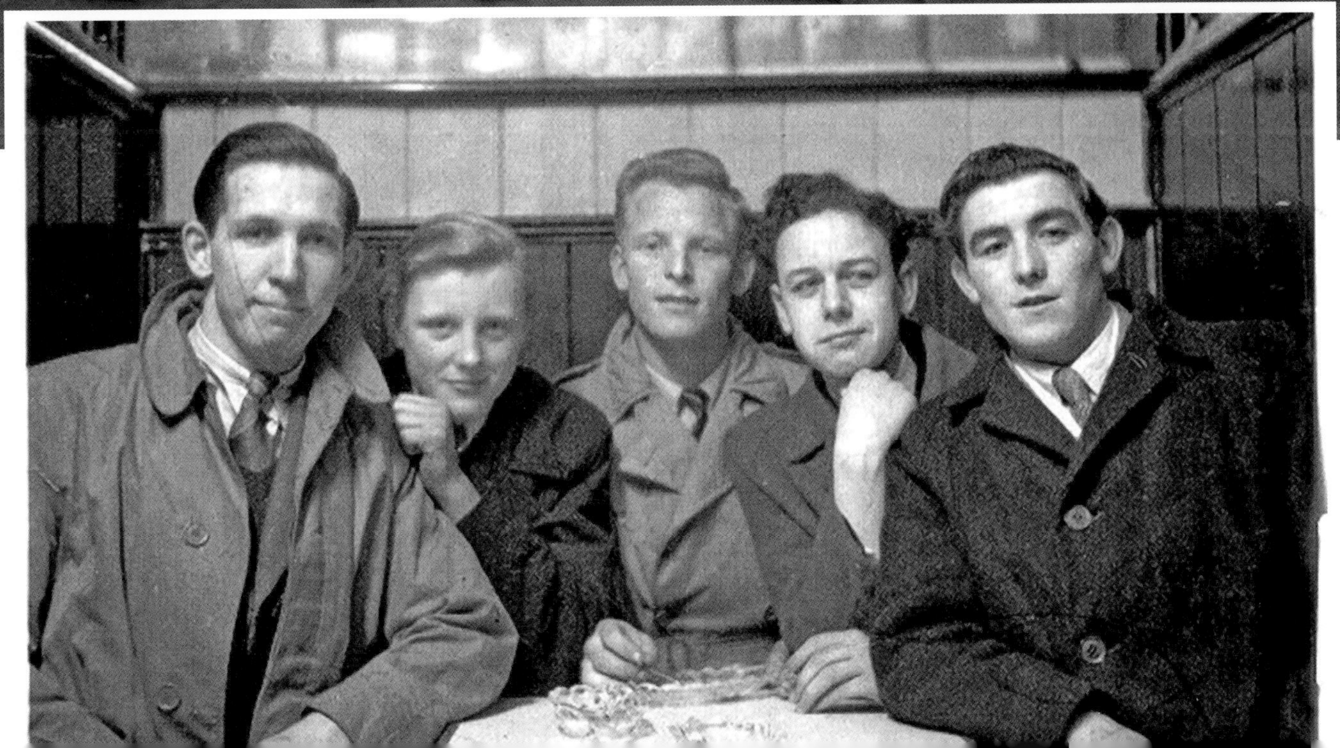

SWANSEA – THIS WAS YOUR LIFE!

This rare gathering of Swansea's Italian cafe owners came about at the wedding of two of them, Augusto Demarco and Assunta Melerangi, in December 1937. They are, from the left: Dom and Ada Pelosi of the Empire Cafe, Nelson Street; Leonard Demarco of Danygraig, St Thomas; Raphael Demarco, father of the groom, Cwmbwrla Cafe; Elfina Demarco, who later married Eric Valerio of Valerio's Cafe, St Helen's Road; the bride and groom of Gus's Cafe in Cwmbwrla; Arnold Demarco, who had a cafe at Carmarthen Road, Waun Wen; Emily Demarco, who ran a cafe at Eversley Road, Sketty; Reggie Demarco, of the cafe at Brynhyfryd Square and Eric Valerio, of St Helen's Road.

Members of the Men's Guild of Terrace Road Chapel, enjoy a spot of hi-jinks at a get togehter at the chapel, early 1960s.

Members of the Womens' Support Group of Uplands St John Ambulance Brigade with officers in charge of the Swansea district, early 1950s.

Staff of newspaper wholesalers Wymans, based at High Street, enjoy an evening out during the early 1960s.

SWANSEA – THIS WAS YOUR LIFE!

Young women members of New Siloh Chapel, Landore, on a caravan holiday in Oxwich, 1958.

Students at the metallurgy department, Swansea University, with their tutors 1958.

A group of Swansea women on a Rock'n'Roll dance night out to Porthcawl in the 1960s. The night was one of many organised by the late Mrs Tegwen Davies.

Typists from the education department at Swansea Guild Hall enjoy a lunchtime stroll in the sunshine, early 1960s.

Members of Waunarlwydd Womens' Institute during a concert, late 1960s.

SWANSEA – THIS WAS YOUR LIFE!

Roy Bevan and his bride with attendants after getting married at Sketty Baptist Church, 1964.

Members and partners of Manselton Social Club at a Christmas dinner and dance held at the Stradey Park Hotel, Llanelli, 1985.

FAMILIAR FACES

Members of Swansea Council's licensing committee leaving the Albert Hall Cinema after a censorship screening of the controversial film Last Tango in Paris, 1972.

Retired staff of the Unit Superheater & Pipe Company of The Strand during a re-union, mid-1970s.

SWANSEA – THIS WAS YOUR LIFE!

Wales, Swansea, Leeds and Juventus football legend John Charles with a group of Swansea women at a charity polo match, 1990.

Members of the West Glamorgan Motor Neurone charity committee with the then Duchess of York, Sarah Ferguson who was a special guest at one of their fundraising dinners in the 1990s.

FAMILIAR FACES

Members of St Thomas Camera Club at its annual awards presentation which followed the club's annual general meeting, 1981.

Anthea Lemonheigh of Treboeth, who bravely fought motor neurone disease with her husband Ernie and friends on the QE2 during a cruise, 1994. As a salute to her battle against illness Anthea was awarded the title of Woman of the Year by West Glamorgan Council for Voluntary Service.

SWANSEA – THIS WAS YOUR LIFE!

Former US President Jimmy Carter who was president of the International Year of Literature hosted by Swansea in 1995 with city councillor Alan Lloyd, the event's chairman, and other officials at Ty Llen, 1995.

The Archbishop of Canterbury, Dr Rowan Williams, on a visit to Oystermouth Castle, 2002.

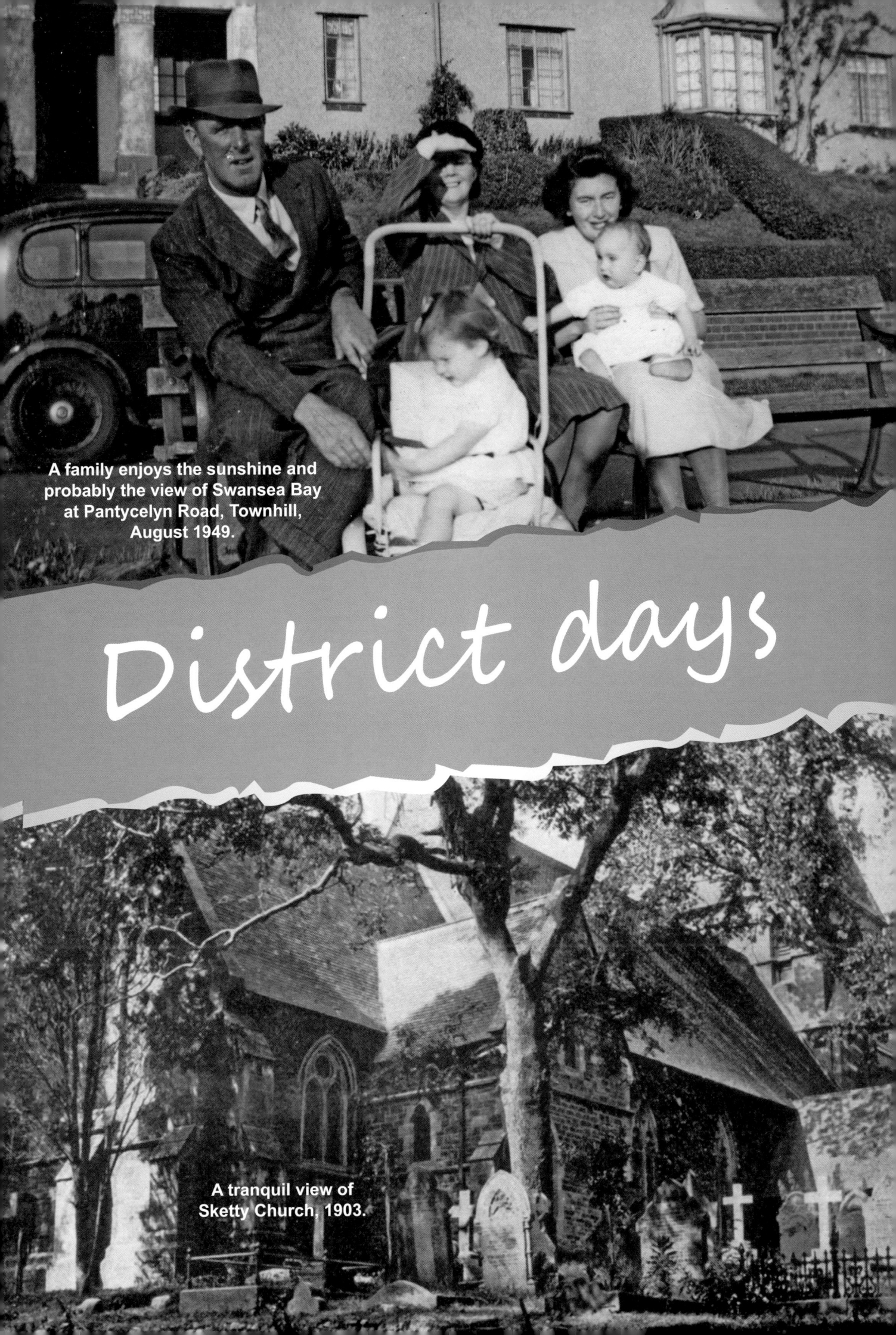

A family enjoys the sunshine and probably the view of Swansea Bay at Pantycelyn Road, Townhill, August 1949.

District days

A tranquil view of Sketty Church, 1903.

SWANSEA – THIS WAS YOUR LIFE!

The gardens at Victoria Park, St Helen's, 1910.

Cwmdonkin Park, Uplands, early 1900s.

DISTRICT DAYS

Rowing boats at the edge of Brynmill Park Lake, 1903. It was originally built as a reservoir, but that use may have ceased by this date.

A tram makes its way along Eversley Road, Sketty. 1920.

Looking westwards across Fforestfach, mid-1930s.

A young boy flies his kite on Star Bank, Fforestfach, mid-1930s. The Star Inn on Carmarthen Road can be seen in the bottom left. The farmland in the distance became Ravenhill Park.

Looking westwards across Fforestfach, mid-1930s.

A white coated policeman stands on traffic point duty at Sketty Cross, in the late-1930s. There were far fewer vehicles on the roads then. Traffic lights perform his task today.

A young mother proudly shows off her young baby near Ivy Bush Court, St Thomas late 1940s. These were some of the original houses in the district. This spot is now the car park behind

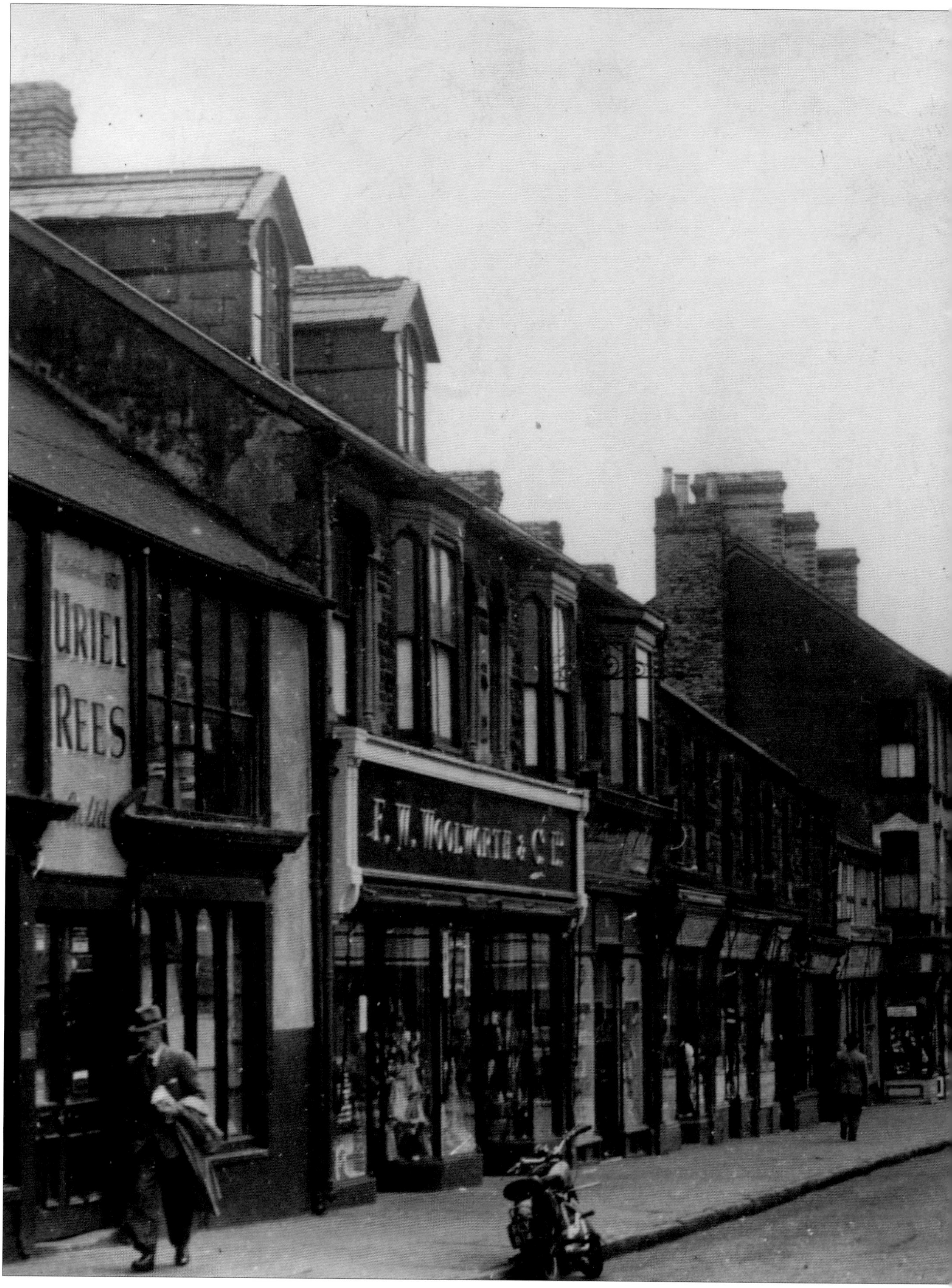
URIEL
REES
F. W. WOOLWORTH & Co. Ltd.

Woodfield Street, Morriston, 1958. The domed building was formerly the Opera House and later a cinema.

A youngster having fun in the snow on his sleigh at Ravenhiill Park during the winter of 1947.

Looking across to Landore and Townhill, from Kilvey Hill, 1967. Breaking the skyline from the left are: Penlan School, now Bryntawe Welsh School, Penlan water tower, and the DVLA building. Landore railway viaduct cuts across the centre of the view.

Boots store and the Marquis Arms at Fforestfach Cross, after a snowfall, December 1950.

The old cinema in Uplands, early 1950s.

A view eastwards through the towering arches of Landore viaduct which carries the main Swansea to Paddington railway line in and out of the city, early 1970s.

DISTRICT DAYS

The junction of Maes Street and Port Tennant Road, St Thomas, 1958.

Fabian Street at its junction with Sebastopol Street, St Thomas, 1963. This is now Fabian Way.

SWANSEA – THIS WAS YOUR LIFE!

Fforestfach Cross, early 1980s.

A view up the River Tawe towards Landore from Foxhole Road, St Thomas, 1981.

Looking through the gated Brynmill Lane entrance to Singleton Park, mid-1960s.

The now closed St Thomas School stands proud among surrounding homes in this view from the top of the BT tower, early 1980s.

Mandinam, the house once occupied by Mr and Mrs JT Morgan at Gower Road, Killay. It was dismantled piece by piece in April, 1992 and parts of it used in the construction of other properties. The site is now occupied by a housing development.

Springfield Street, Morriston, after overnight snow, February, 1993.

DISTRICT DAYS

The early operating depot of Morris Bros coaches, Port Tennant Road, Port Tennant, mid-1960s.

Looking towards the beach through the arch of the Swansea to Shrewsbury railway line at Brynmill during a high tide in August 1967.

Morris Lane School, St Thomas, 1969.

Gabalfa Road, Sketty in the snow, February 9, 1969.

Deserted blocks of flats at Sketty Park just before they were demolished, November 16, 2003.

Kevin Johns heads up a cast of young pirates for a performance that formed part of the unveiling of the SA1 development, September 30, 2006.

The performers

Chorus members of Uplands Arts Club's performance of the Gilbert & Sullivan operetta, Yeoman of the Guard, 1957.

A production underway at the New Star Theatre, Wind Street, 1903.

Members of the Swansea Imperial Octet, 1938.

Members of the Swansea Imperial Singers, 1938.

The cast of She Stoops to Conquer, a play staged by pupils of Swansea High School, later known as Llwyn y Bryn School, January 1950.

Participants in the Christmas pantomime at New Siloh Chapel, Landore, 1952.

Members of the Swansea Corps of the Women's Junior Air Corps band who took part in a Festival of Britain rally in London, June 9, 1951.

Members of Einon Baptist Chapel, Morriston, perform the Nativity, Christmas 1956.

Pupils of Swansea Girls' High School, take part in Chronicle, staged to celebrate its 60th anniversary, February 1949.

Swansea Male Voice Choir with organist Reginald Foot pictured before a performance in the city, late 1930s.

Clwyd School Choir, 1958, with teacher and conductor, Miss Evans.

Edward and Nina Newton of the Edward Newton School of Dancing, early 1950s.

SWANSEA – THIS WAS YOUR LIFE!

Social club members of the Lewis Lewis department store, High Street, during a performance of Aladdin in the staff canteen, early 1950s.

Members of the Hazel Johnson School of Dance, 1985.

The cast of Swansea amateur Operatic Society's production of Oliver at the Grand Theatre, 1996.

The percussion band of Danygraig Junior Mixed School, winners in the National Eisteddfod, 1956.

Members of Brynhyfryd Solitaires kazoo band, 1974.

The Aeolian Singers, 1972.

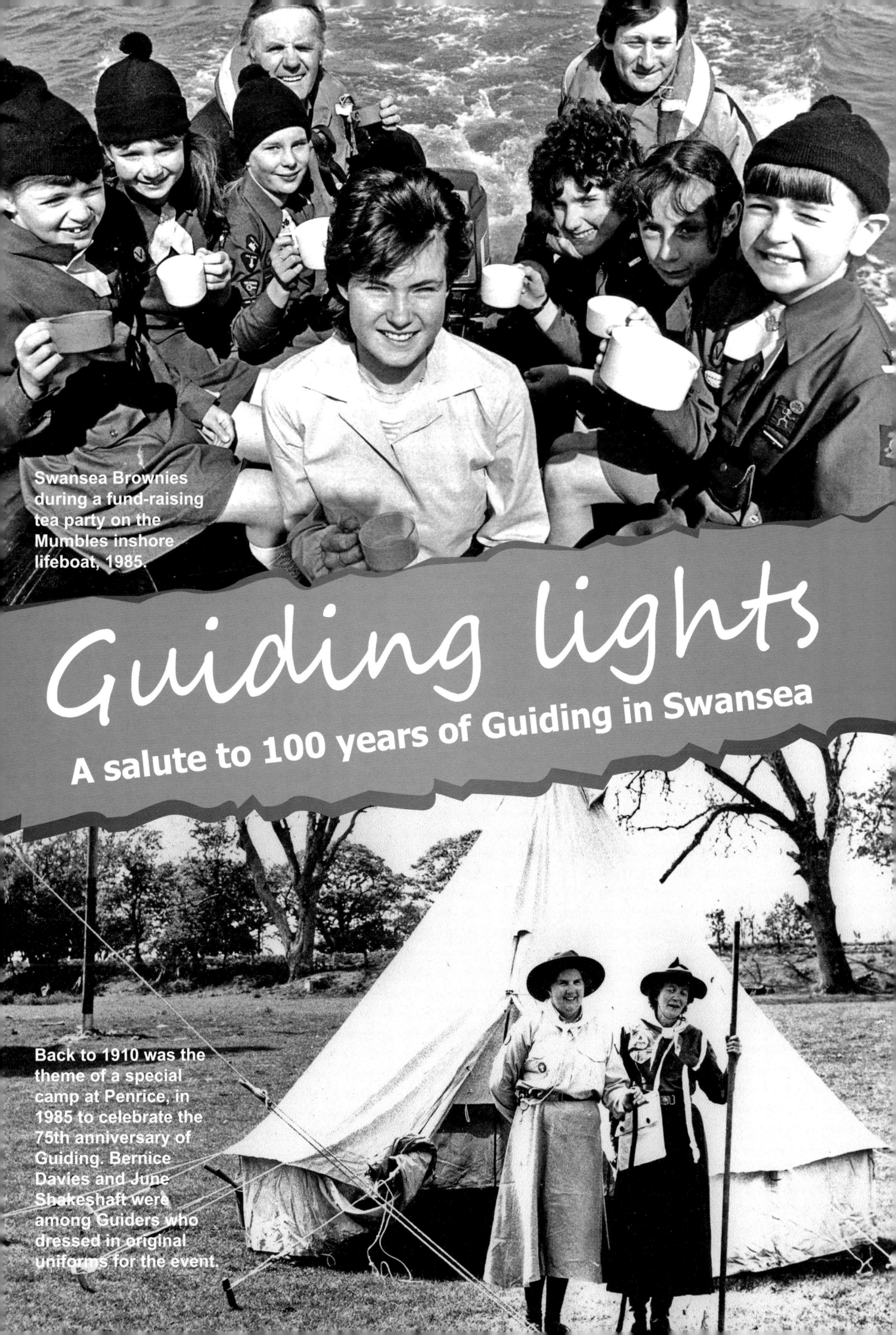

Swansea Brownies during a fund-raising tea party on the Mumbles inshore lifeboat, 1985.

Guiding lights
A salute to 100 years of Guiding in Swansea

Back to 1910 was the theme of a special camp at Penrice, in 1985 to celebrate the 75th anniversary of Guiding. Bernice Davies and June Shakeshaft were among Guiders who dressed in original uniforms for the event.

Swansea Guides at camp in Oxwich, 1930. Bell tents were the order of the day then.

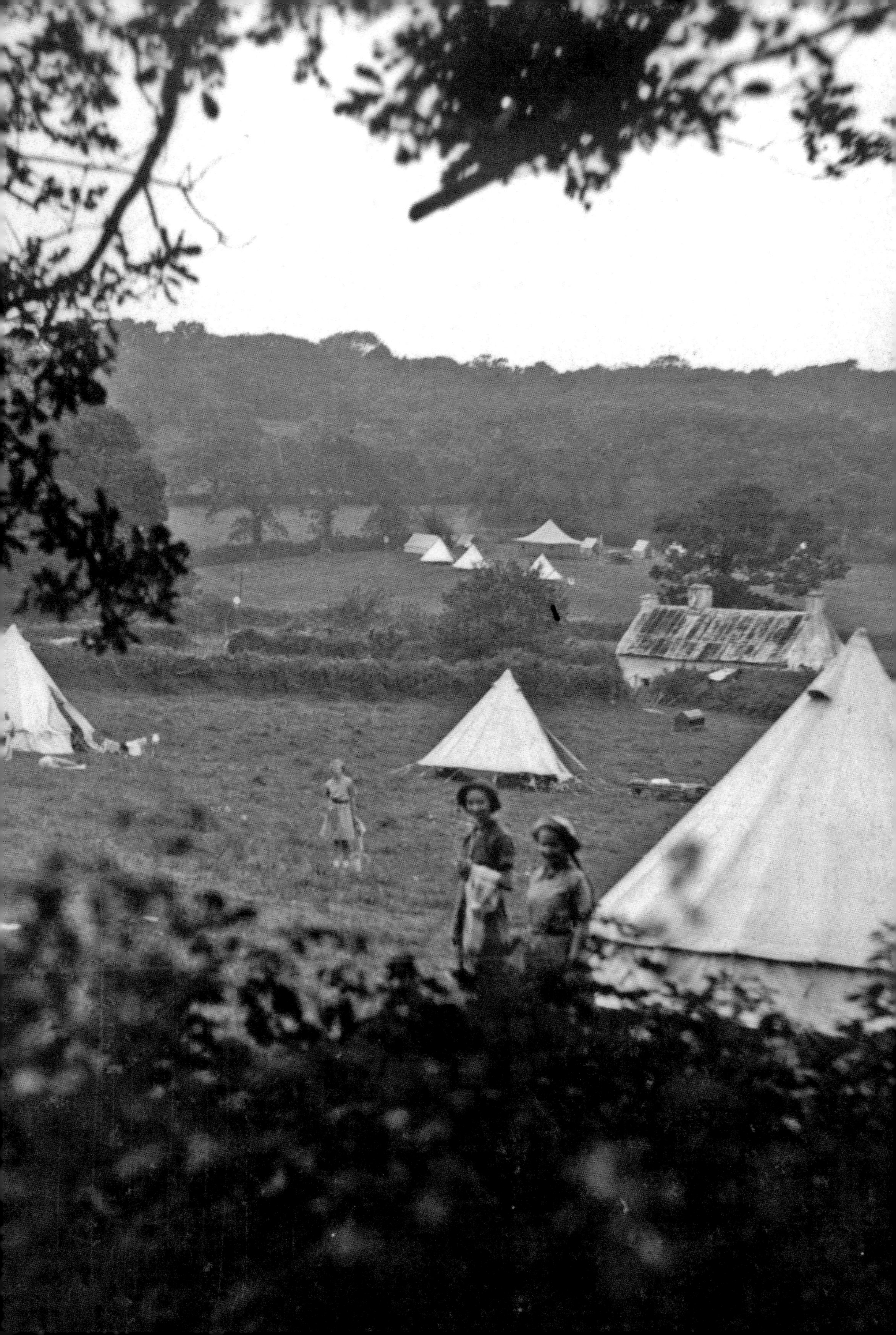

A group of Swansea Guides at camp, 1928.

Guides demonstrating their first aid skills before the Princess Royal at Singleton Park, 1932. Looking on are Lady Davies, Chief Commissioner for Guides in Wales and other Welsh commissioners.

SWANSEA – THIS WAS YOUR LIFE!

Swansea St Mary's Guide Company, 1933.

Camping, 1934-style for these adventurous Swansea Guides.

The 1st Parkmill and Penmaen Guide Company together with Brownies outside the Gower Inn, Parkmill, together with Mrs Morris, landlady, mid-1940s.

Members of the Mount Pleasant and YWCA Guide Companies, combine to pack comfort parcels for troops during the Second World War, 1940.

SWANSEA – THIS WAS YOUR LIFE!

Members of the 1st Bonymaen Guide Company, winners of the coveted Swansea Divisional proficiency trophy, late 1940s.

Guides of the 1st Blackpill and Mumbles companies enjoy some fun and games at their annual Christmas party at the Vivian Hall, Blackpill, 1952.

Swansea Ranger Guides in Penrice, Gower, late 1950s.

Members of the 1st Blackpill Guides practice their debating skills with company Captain, Jean Gilbert, 1952.

A patrol of the 4th Swansea, St David's Roman Catholic Church Guides, 1954.

Swansea Guides at a summer camp in Lawrenny, Pembrokeshire, 1968.

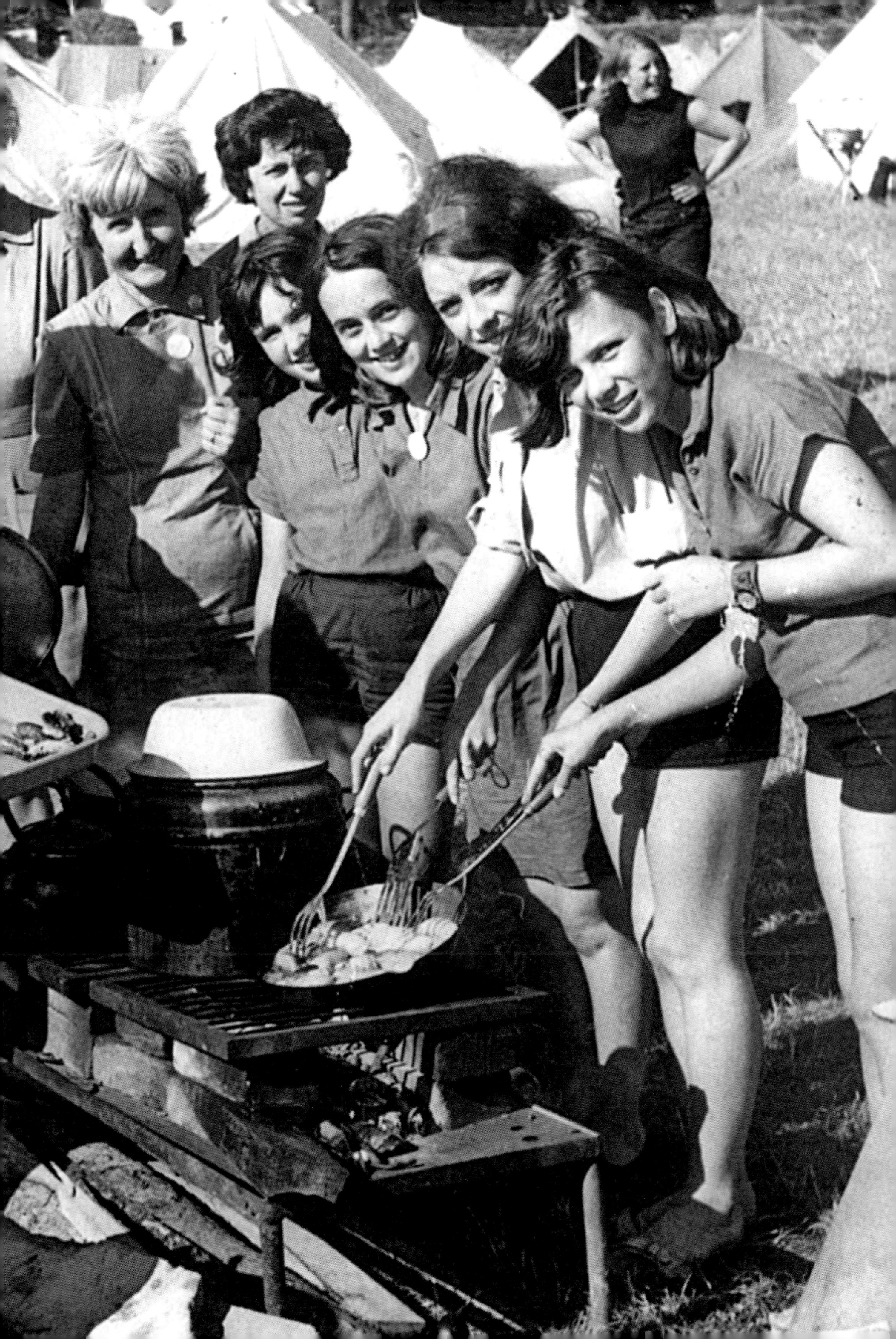

A knot-making class run by Captain Jean Gilbert at the 1st Blackpill Guide headquarters, 1952.

Members of Swansea St James Guide Company at summer camp in Llanmadoc, Gower, 1955.

All Souls, Tycoch, Brownie pack during a fancy dress tea party, 1985. It was held to raise funds for the Welsh Guide headquarters at Broneirion, Powys. Special guest at the event was the city's Mayoress, Jane Murphy.

It was a case of fun in the sun for these Guides as they cool off in a stream at Parkmill during a visit to the West Glamorgan Girl Guides Activity Centre, July, 2007.

SWANSEA – THIS WAS YOUR LIFE!

Some of the Swansea Guide representatives who attended a weekend conference in the city, entitled The Next Step, May, 1966.

Guides, guests and officials witness the cutting of the ribbon that signalled the opening of Penrice Guide Headquarters, 1975.

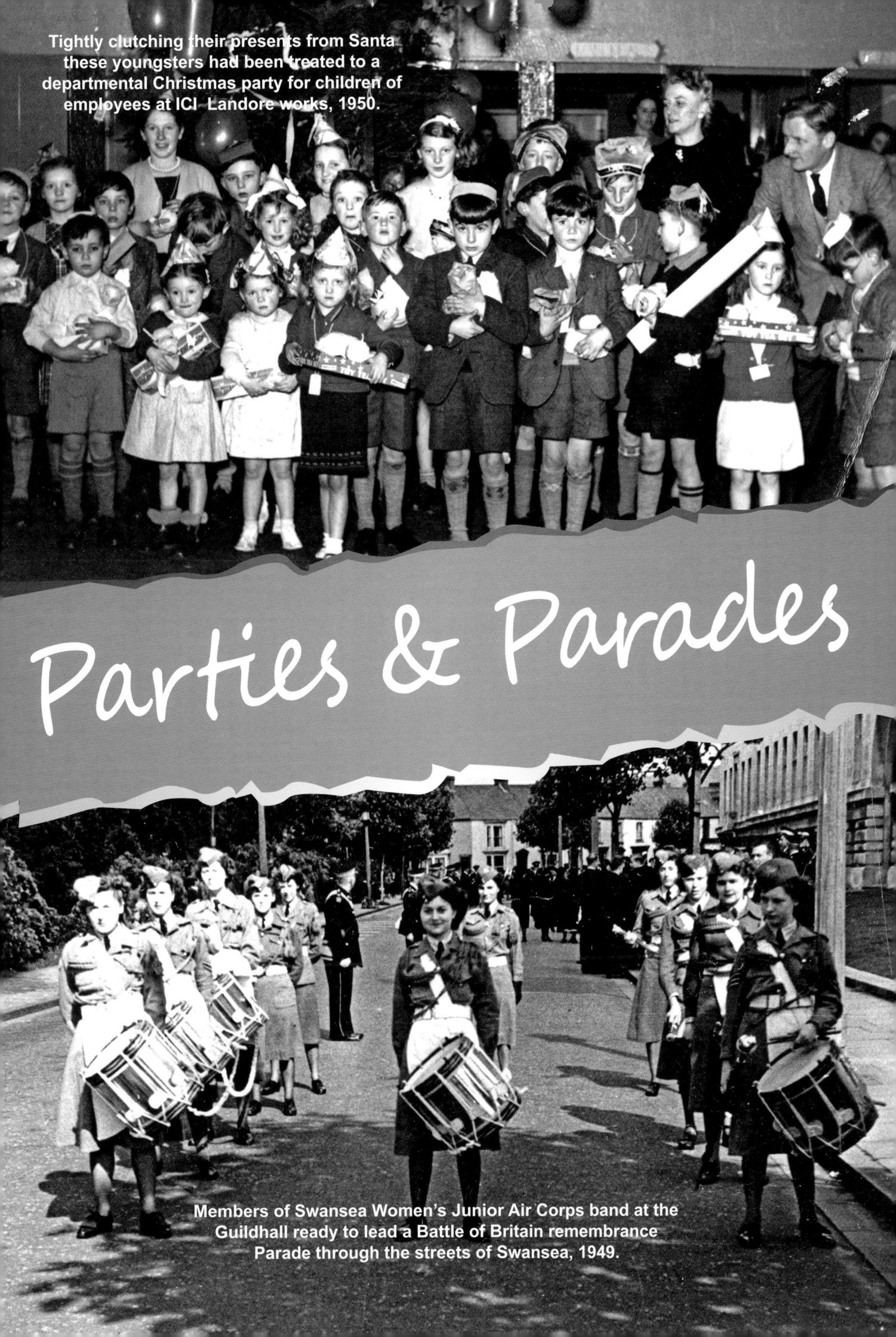

Tightly clutching their presents from Santa these youngsters had been treated to a departmental Christmas party for children of employees at ICI Landore works, 1950.

Parties & Parades

Members of Swansea Women's Junior Air Corps band at the Guildhall ready to lead a Battle of Britain remembrance Parade through the streets of Swansea, 1949.

Office staff of the Lewis Lewis department store, High Street, at their annual Christmas dance, 1950.

This happy group was celebrating the Festival of Britain at Slate Street, Morriston, 1951.

PARTIES & PARADES

Staff of the typing pool at the Education Department at Swansea Guildhall enjoy a celebration dinner, early 1960s.

Some of the staff of Wind Street Post Office, at their annual dinner, 1959.

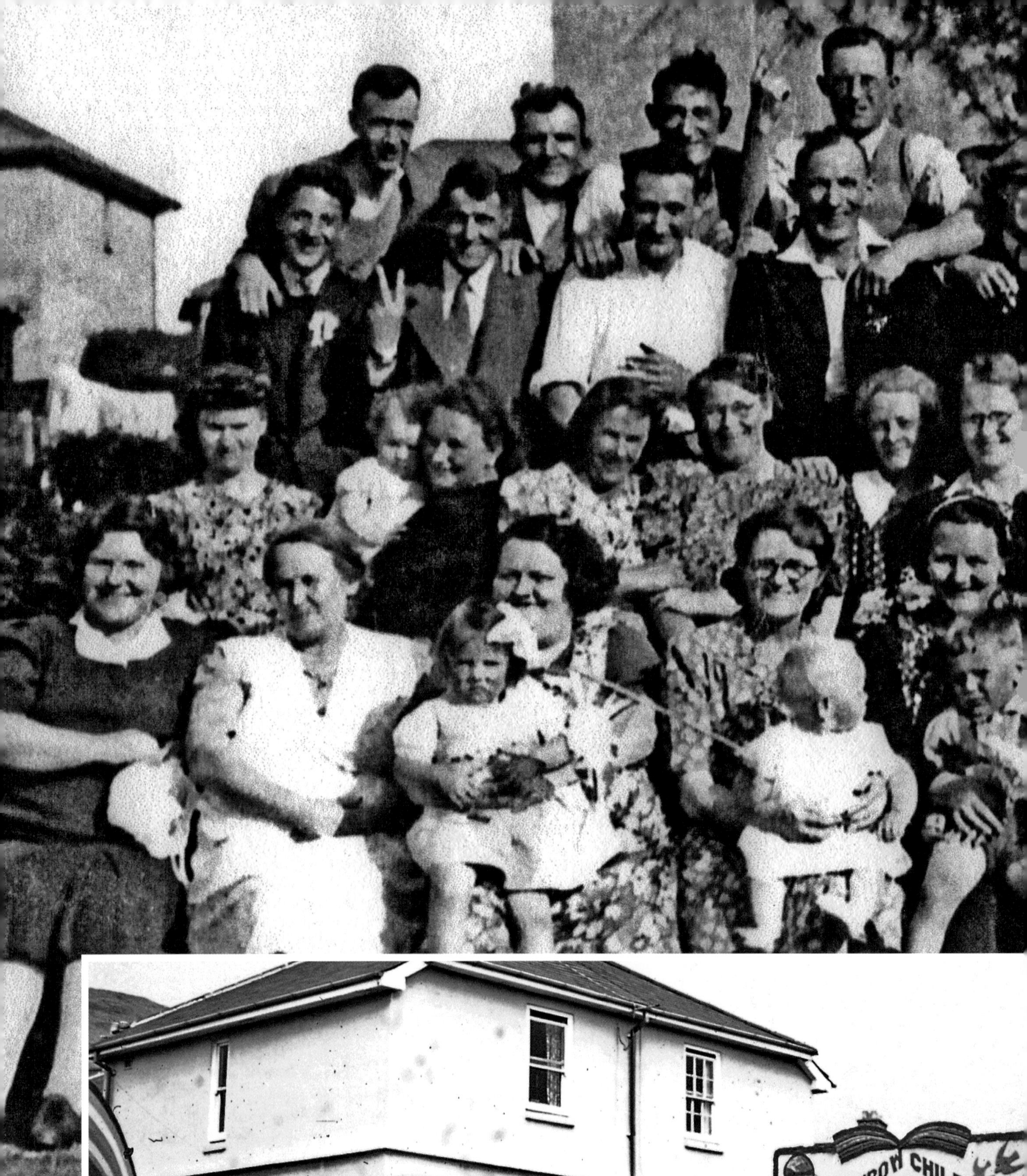

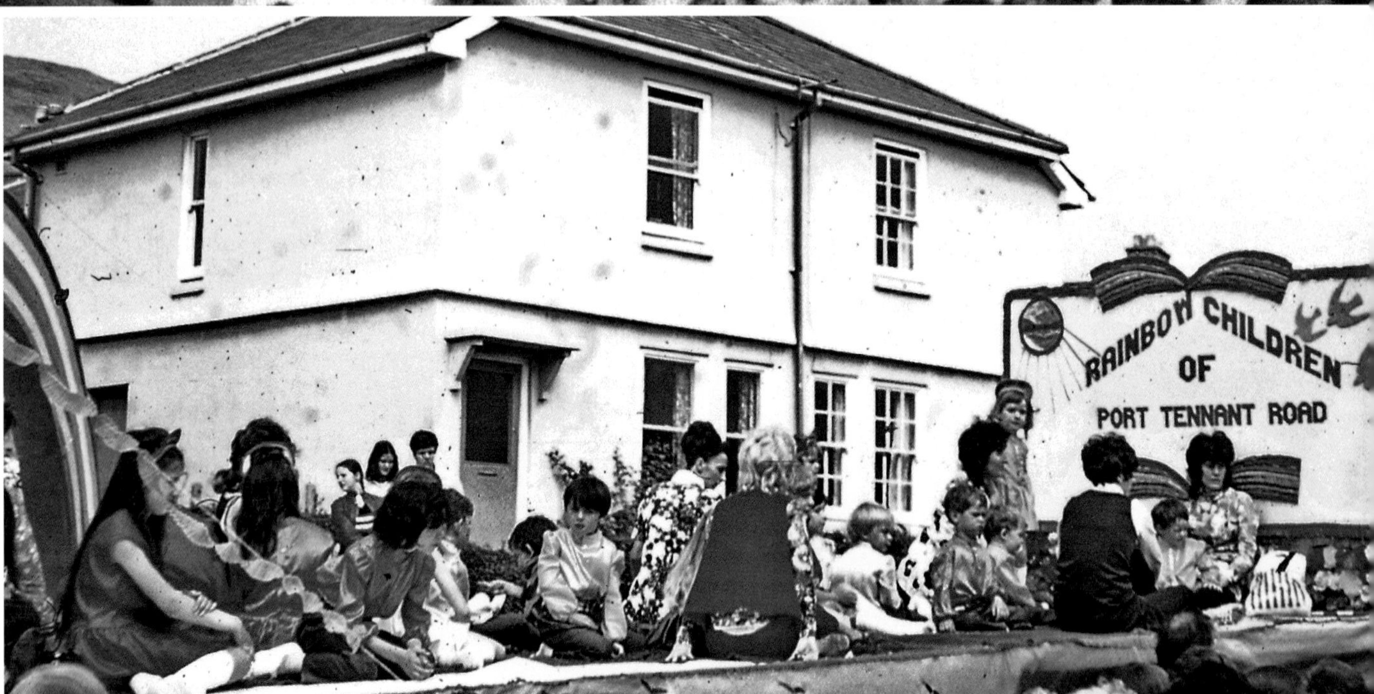
RAINBOW CHILDREN
OF
PORT TENNANT ROAD

Residents of Garden City, Fforestfach during their celebrations to mark VE Day, September, 1945.

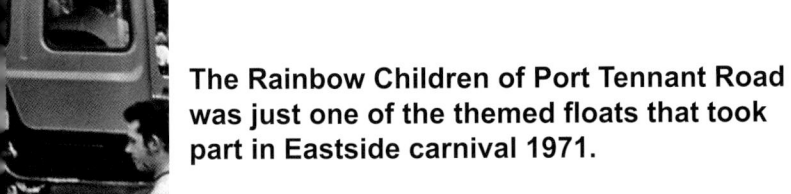

The Rainbow Children of Port Tennant Road was just one of the themed floats that took part in Eastside carnival 1971.

Young members of the Irvine Dance Club, Southend, in fancy dress, 1955.

Staff at Mount Pleasant Geriatric Hospital help one of their patients celebrate her 100th birthday, during the 1970s.

An Easter bonnet parade in the playground of St Thomas Infants School, early 1970s. The school has since closed and been transformed into residential apartments.

Swansea Air Cadet band leads the annual remembrance Day procession along the Kingsway, November 1988.

A group of female BT employees enjoy a night out, 1982.

A fashion parade in the restaurant of David Evans' department store, 1959.

A birthday party held in the now demolished church hall at Kilvey Church, early 1970s.

Staff of the Corgi toy factory, Fforestfach, at a presentation evening for one of their colleagues, mid-1970s.

Women employees of the South Dock Spontex factory at a staff party, mid-1980s.

The Royal cavalcade carrying Prince Charles on his Investiture tour of Wales heads out of Swansea along Fabian Way. Crowds lined his city route and there was a strong roadside police presence, August, 1969.

Eastside's St. Elmo Avenue Yellow Submarine float at Bracelet Bay car park, ready to take part in Mumbles Carnival parade mid 1970s.

SWANSEA – THIS WAS YOUR LIFE!

The Top Rank Suite, Kingsway, was the venue for the Pharmacy Ball attended by this group, November 10, 1972.

A group of workers at Ford's Jersey Marine plant on a Christmas night out, 1972.

Welsh Guards march along St Helen's Road during a Freedom of the City parade through Swansea, September 1982.

A young fatstock handler prepares to show off his charge in one of the cattle classes at the Gower Show, Penrice 2009.

SWANSEA – THIS WAS YOUR LIFE!

Morriston Post Office staff with their partners at a Christmas dinner, 1990.

Members of the organising committee of a Ben Motor Ball held at the Top Rank Suite, Kingsway, with comedian Stan Stennet and Swansea City manager, Trevor Ford, late 1970s.

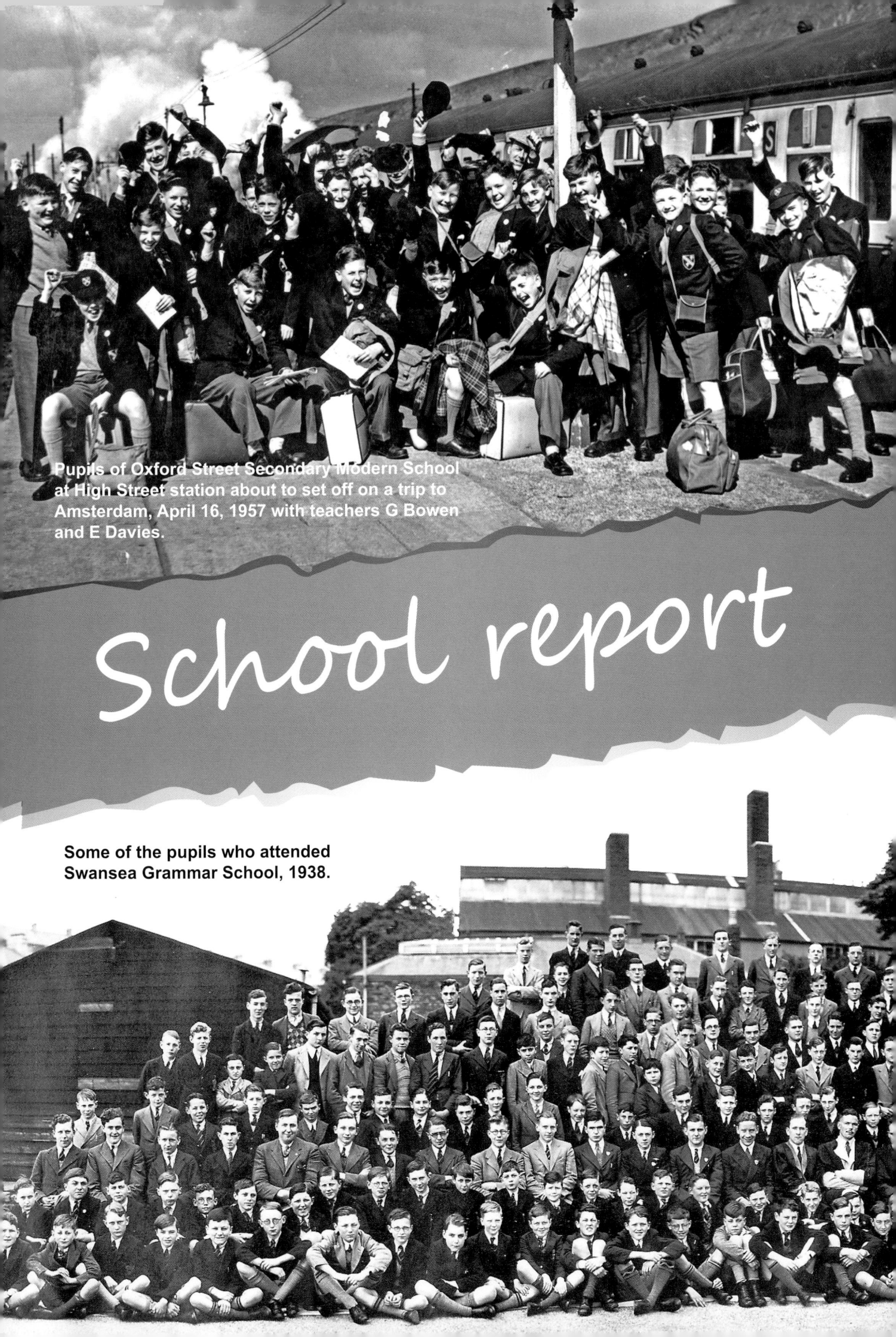

Pupils of Oxford Street Secondary Modern School at High Street station about to set off on a trip to Amsterdam, April 16, 1957 with teachers G Bowen and E Davies.

School report

Some of the pupils who attended Swansea Grammar School, 1938.

Pupils of Manselton Infants School, 1916.

A class at Oxford Street Girls School, 1924.

Pupils of Standard 6, Terrace Road Boys School, 1919.

Standard 3, Oxford Street Boys School, 1932.

The boys of Brynhyfryd Primary School who passed their 11- plus exam in 1949.

Oystermouth Junior School pupils with their teacher and head teacher Albert Williams, 1957.

Pupils at Hafod Primary School, 1949.

A class at Oystermouth Infants School, 1955.

Prefects at Oxford Street Boys School, 1954.

SCHOOL REPORT

Pupils of Lonlas Welsh School, early 1950s.

Fifth form pupils of Llwyn y Bryn Girls School, Uplands, on an educational trip, July 1951.

SWANSEA – THIS WAS YOUR LIFE!

A class of boys at Bishop Gore School, Sketty, 1952.

One of the classes at Hafod Primary School after a PE lesson 1956. The head teacher was Ivor E Sims, who on April 23, 1935 formed Morriston Orpheus Choir.

A class at Bishop Gore Grammar School, Sketty, 1954.

SCHOOL REPORT

A mixed class at Terrace Road Junior School, June 1958.

Form 4B Dynevor School, with their teacher, 1957. The school suffered badly in wartime bombing raids and the buildings in the background were demolished to make way for a new school hall.

Boys at St Thomas School with their teacher and head teacher, 1937.

Class 5A, Dynevor School 1959-60. Headmaster Meredith Hughes is in the centre of the front row.

SCHOOL REPORT

Some of the pupils at Lloyd's School, with their teacher, 1949.

These four youngsters are delighted to be celebrating their last day of school at Townhill, 1960.

A class at Terrace Road Primary School, Townhill, on St Davids Day, with their teacher, 1960.

This group of pupils at Oxford Street Secondary Modern School had gathered together after returning from a trip to Holland, 1957.

SCHOOL REPORT

Class 1A, Penlan Comprehensive School for Boys, with their teacher Mr Morgan, September 1973.

A class of girls at Gorseinon Junior School dressed for St David's Day celebrations, 1976.

Some of the pupils at Plasmarl Junior School, 1976.

A class at Parkland School, Sketty, on July 5, 1973.

Students of Llwyn Y Bryn Girls School's upper sixth General Group, July 1961.

A class of pupils at Hafod Primary School, 1982.

SWANSEA – THIS WAS YOUR LIFE!

Pupils of Tutor group 4F2, Morriston Senior Comprehensive School, Cwmrhydyceirw, with teachers, 1978.

Pupils of Plasmarl Infants School during its Nativity performance December 1995.

SCHOOL REPORT

Forms 2 & 3 Pentrehafod Lower School, 1979.

Pupils at Oystermouth Junior School, 1958.

A group of pupils of Swansea Technical School which was housed for a time at the old Guildhall, now Ty Llen. They are seen in the front courtyard, mid-1950s.

St David's Day at Parkland Primary School, Sketty, 1973.

A gathering of motorcyclists and behind them motorists at Bracelet Bay, early 1900s. It is likely that they were taking part in an early motor rally.

Moving along

Cargo vessels berthed in a crowded Prince of Wales Dock, 1910.

A double deck tram bound for Brynmill heads down Oxford Street, 1910.

A group of Swansea day trippers about to set off on a charabanc outing, late 1920s.

A single deck tramcar emerges into Quay Parade from under the Cuba bridge of the high level railway line that connected the King's and Prince of Wales Docks with the South Dock, 1930.

Ferryboat men on the River Tawe, near White Rock, early 1900s. This was a vital way of crossing the river here for many people.

The Mumbles train at the Slip, on a late summer's afternoon, 1921. The Bay View Hotel is on the left. The shadow of the Slip Bridge can be seen on the road.

A six-wheeled 1939 AEC Renown single deck bus heads down Castle Street on its way to Langland Bay, 1949. Route 85 took it through Sketty, Blackpill and Mumbles.

Mumbles Head provided the backdrop for this late 1940s line up of the delivery fleet of John Jones' Mumbles Dairy. The four battery electric floats were manufactured by Morrison-Electricar The petrol pick-up alongside them is a late 1930s Austin 12.

This RAF vehicle was used to tether a barrage balloon at Grenfell Park, St Thomas during the Second World War.

Sailing vessels loading and waiting their turn in the Prince of Wales Dock. Their cargo was anthracite coal bound for San Francisco in the United States.

Looking across a busy South Dock, filled with sailing vessels, 1903.

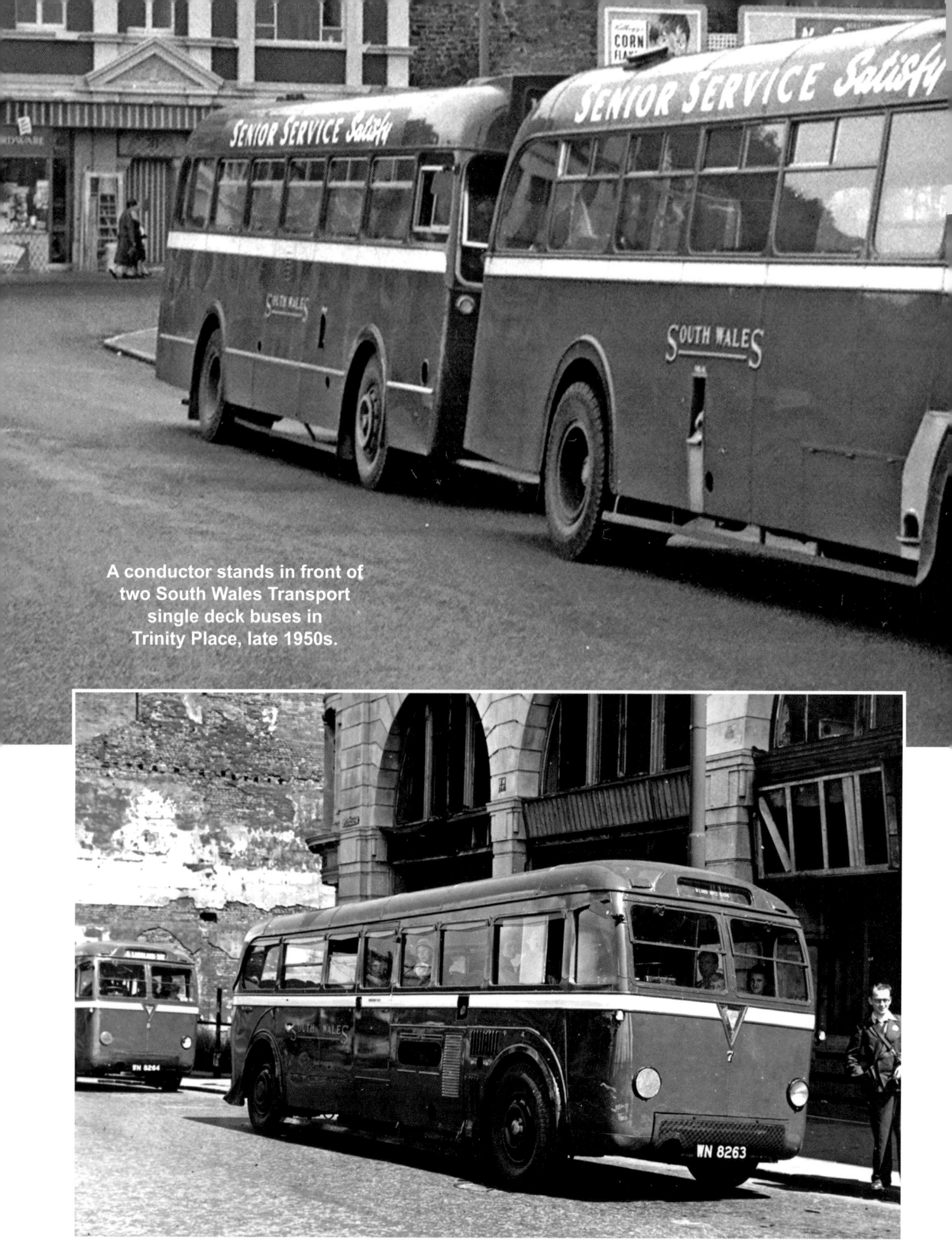

A conductor stands in front of two South Wales Transport single deck buses in Trinity Place, late 1950s.

Two of five AEC Q-type buses bought for Townhill use by the South Wales Transport company wait at the kerbside alongside buildings in Castle Street, 1936. They served the company until 1949.

A six-wheeled, Brush-bodied, 1939 AEC Renown half cab bus used on busy Townhill routes by the South Wales Transport bus company until 1949.

Crowds throng the shoreline at Porteynon on the afternoon of August 3, 1981, after the steamer Prince Ivanhoe struck rocks in the bay and was grounded. A full scale operation swung into action to rescue passengers from the packed vessel. Here the crew of an inflatable craft are towing a large, covered inflatable liferaft full of passengers off the ill-fated vessel.

A family patiently awaits rescue from the stricken paddle steamer Prince Ivanhoe after it ran aground.

A lifeboat is lowered from the Prince Ivanhoe as an inflatable craft with its crew pulls alongside to help.

136

The incoming tide begins to claim the 30-year-old Prince Ivanhoe.

Lifejackets were quickly put to use as the steamer was beached at Porteynon. The only casualty of the incident was a man who died of a heart attack during the rescue.

The Prince Ivanhoe succumbs to the incoming tide. She was grounded at Porteynon after ripping a 60 foot gash in her hull on rocks in the bay on August 3, 1981.

One of the excavators used at Swansea Brickworks, Cwmdu, mid-1940s.

A load of timber frames for housing leaves the North Dock depot of British Road Services on an articulated AEC lorry, 1960.

Lorries lined up at British Road Services North Dock depot, Sunday November 6, 1960.

CHAPTER

A signalman surveys the highly polished banks of levers at Kings Dock Signal box, June 1987.

Burrows Sidings signal box, near Crymlyn Burrows, June 1987. The bridge in the distance carries the busy Fabian Way dual carriageway.

An array of appliances lined up in front of Swansea's main fire station, Grove Place, 2000. Among them at least one vintage machine.

The Swansea-Cork ferry Innisfallen lifts her bow door as she heads for the River Tawe Ferryport, mid-1970s. The vessel had been introduced in May, 1969 and remained in service until 1978.

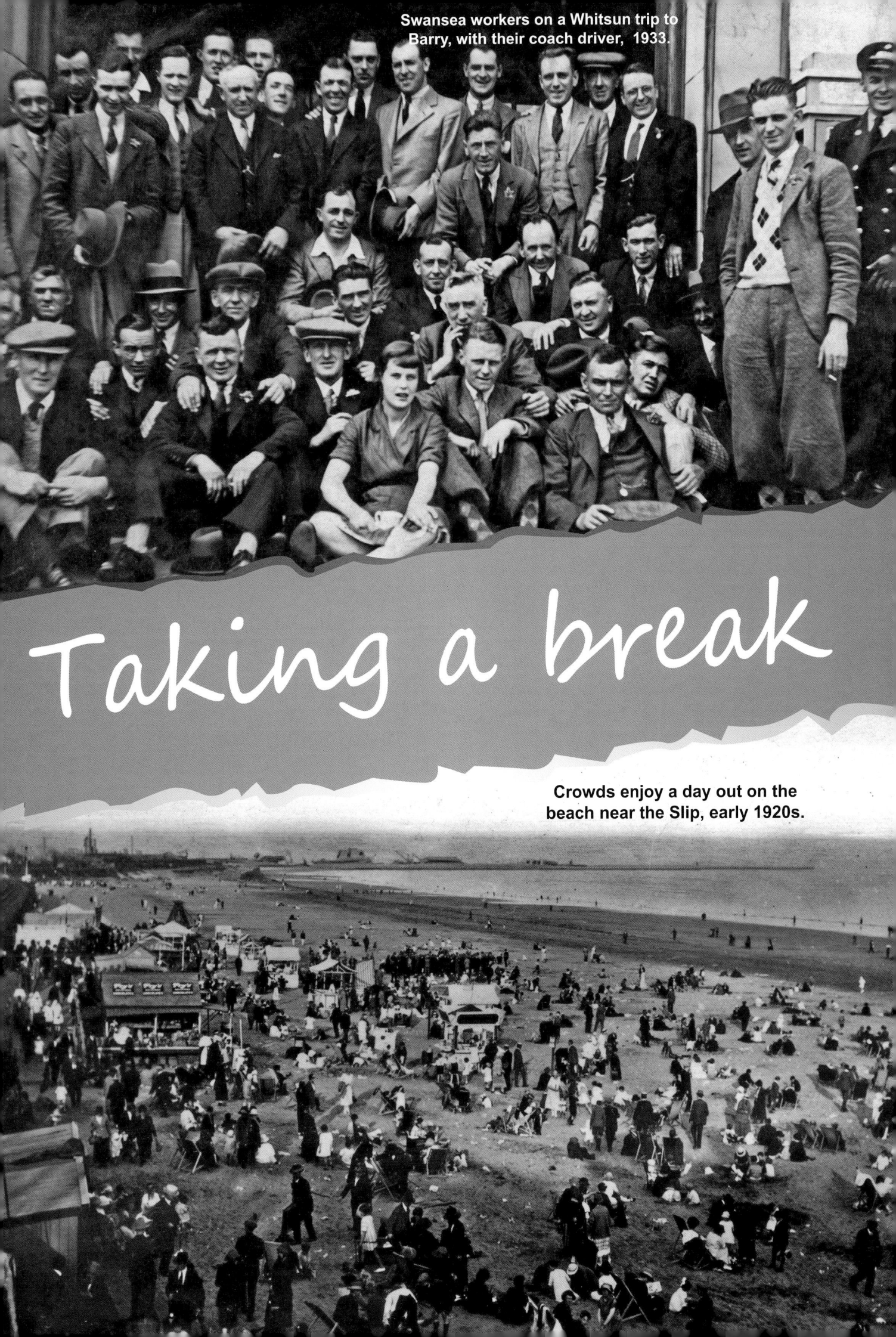

Swansea workers on a Whitsun trip to Barry, with their coach driver, 1933.

Taking a break

Crowds enjoy a day out on the beach near the Slip, early 1920s.

SWANSEA – THIS WAS YOUR LIFE!

Youngsters take time out from having fun on Swansea Beach, late 1940s.

A bucket and spade meant sandcastle time on the sands at The Slip, 1950.

Employees of Richard Thomas & Baldwin's Landore works on an outing, late 1940s.

BREAK TIME

A group of Swansea men all set for a day out, early 1950s.

Staff of Hodges menswear factory, Kingsway Industrial Estate, Fforestfach, on a day trip, 1950.

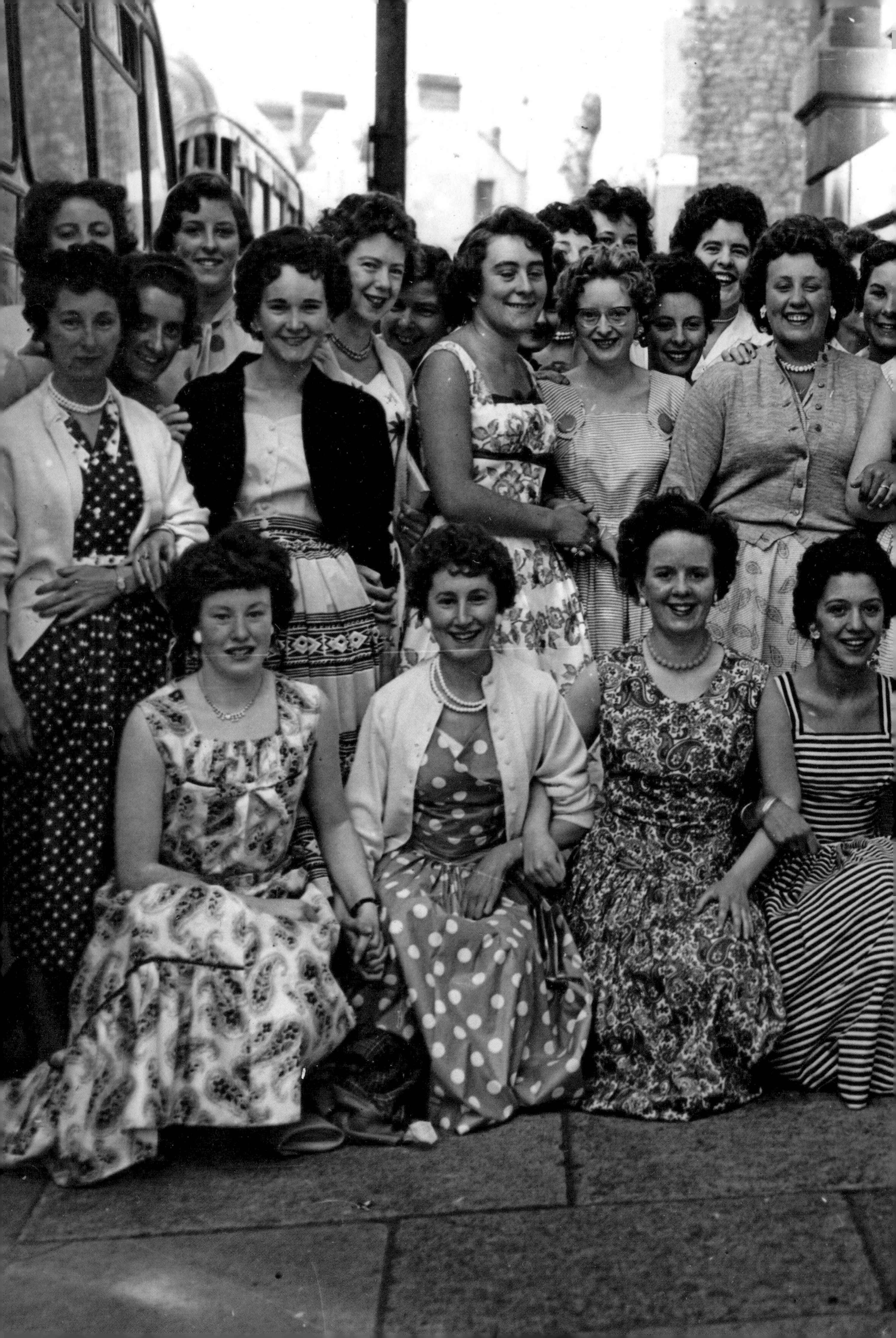

Staff of Lewis Lewis store, High Street, gather before setting off for a day trip to Llanwrtyd Wells, mid-1950s.

SWANSEA – THIS WAS YOUR LIFE!

Four young Swansea lads enjoy a trip to Ilfracombe aboard the steamer Glen Gower.

A group of Dunvant residents on a trip to London during the Festival of Britain, 1951.

All set for their annual day out at Chepstow Races are these members of the Labour Club, Wind Street, mid-1980s. They would have lunch in the Kings Hotel, Newport, go to the races, return to the Kings Hotel for more food and then go on to the Dockers' Club in Newport for the evening before heading back to Swansea.

Four women from Aberdyberthi Street on a seaside day trip, late 1950s.

A group of Hafod residents on a summertime coach trip, mid-1950s.

Swansea and West Glamorgan councillors join other dignitaries to take a miniature train ride around one of the displays during a civic visit to the National Garden Festival held at Ebbw Vale, 1991.

A group of Swansea GPO telephonists on a day out in Shrewsbury, 1960.

Staff of the Albert Hall Cinema about to set off on a coach trip, mid-1950s.

SWANSEA – THIS WAS YOUR LIFE!

Crowds watch a daredevil motorcycle stunt rider perform his fiery spectacle at the City & County of Swansea Show, Singleton Park, May 28, 2007.

Members of the Eagle Inn's womens darts team during a weekend away early 1990s.

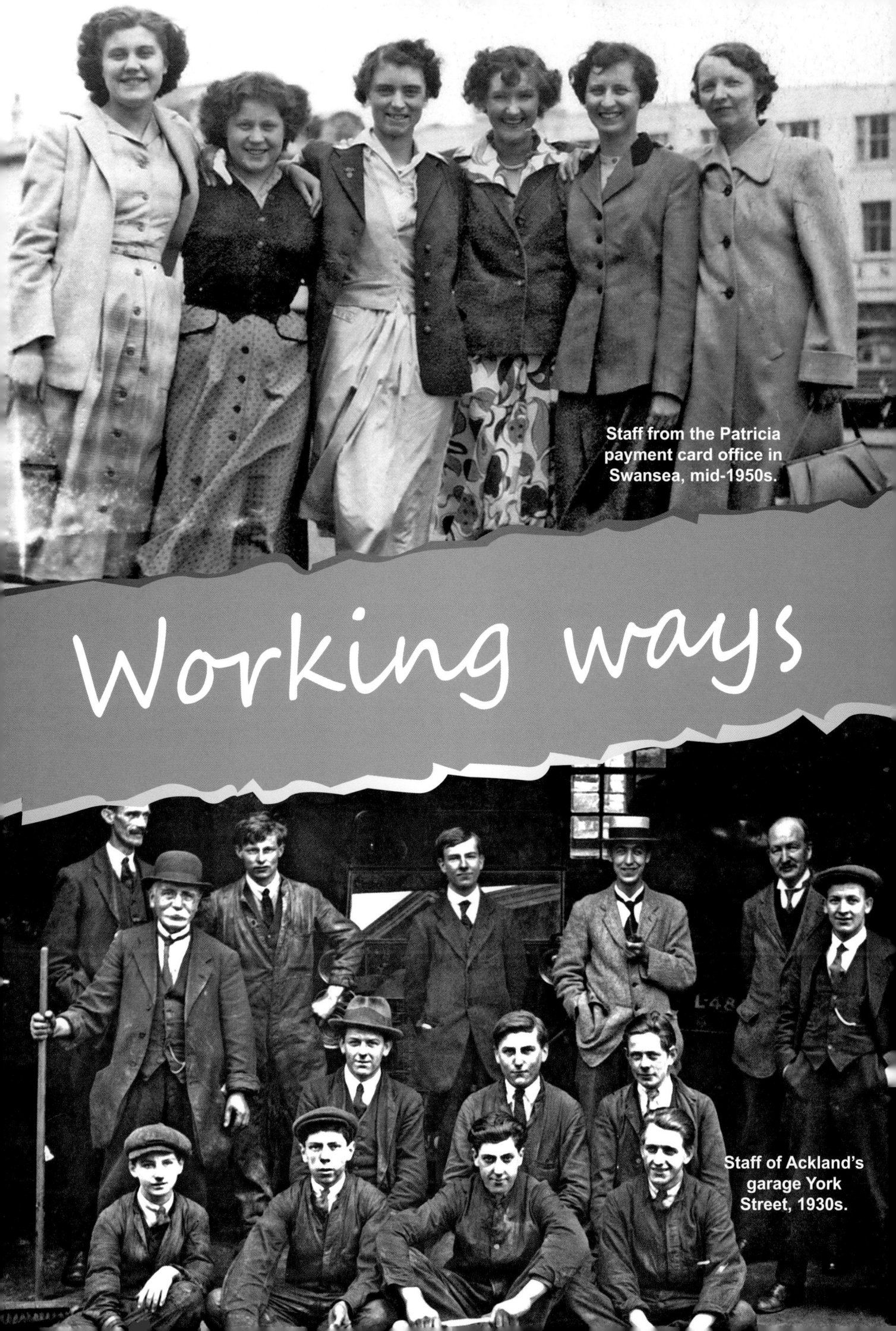

Staff from the Patricia payment card office in Swansea, mid-1950s.

Working ways

Staff of Ackland's garage York Street, 1930s.

Bill Williams, a baker at Bert's Bakery, Recorder Street, Sandfields, with an assistant, 1940.

Three bakery workers at Hafod, 1930.

Betts mineral water works, Northampton Lane, Swansea, 1903.

The fish wharves and market, at Swansea Docks, 1903.

Workmates at Cwmfelin Tinplate Works, June 19, 1937.

SWANSEA – THIS WAS YOUR LIFE!

A workman engaged in building a wall at Swansea Brickworks, Cwmdu, mid-1940s.

WORKING WAYS

Crowds of factory workers and onlookers gather to catch a glimpse of King George VI when he visited Swansea to officially open the new Mettoy factory at Fforestfach, on April 2, 1949. Every vantage point was taken, including balconies and surrounding factory rooftops.

Young women workers of the Premier Clothing Supply Company take a break from their labours on the roof of their office, 1955.

Supervisors at the Northgate clothing factory, Fforestfach in the mid-1970s. The factory ceased operation in 1980.

Some of the staff of the Planning Department of Swansea County Borough Council in the former St Faith's Church opposite the Guildhall where the department was housed throughout the 1950s.

Women outside the South Dock Spontex factory where they worked during the 1970s.

Staff of Woolworths Oxford Street store outside the building, mid-1930s. Nothing in these stores over sixpence, proclaimed the sign across the frontage.

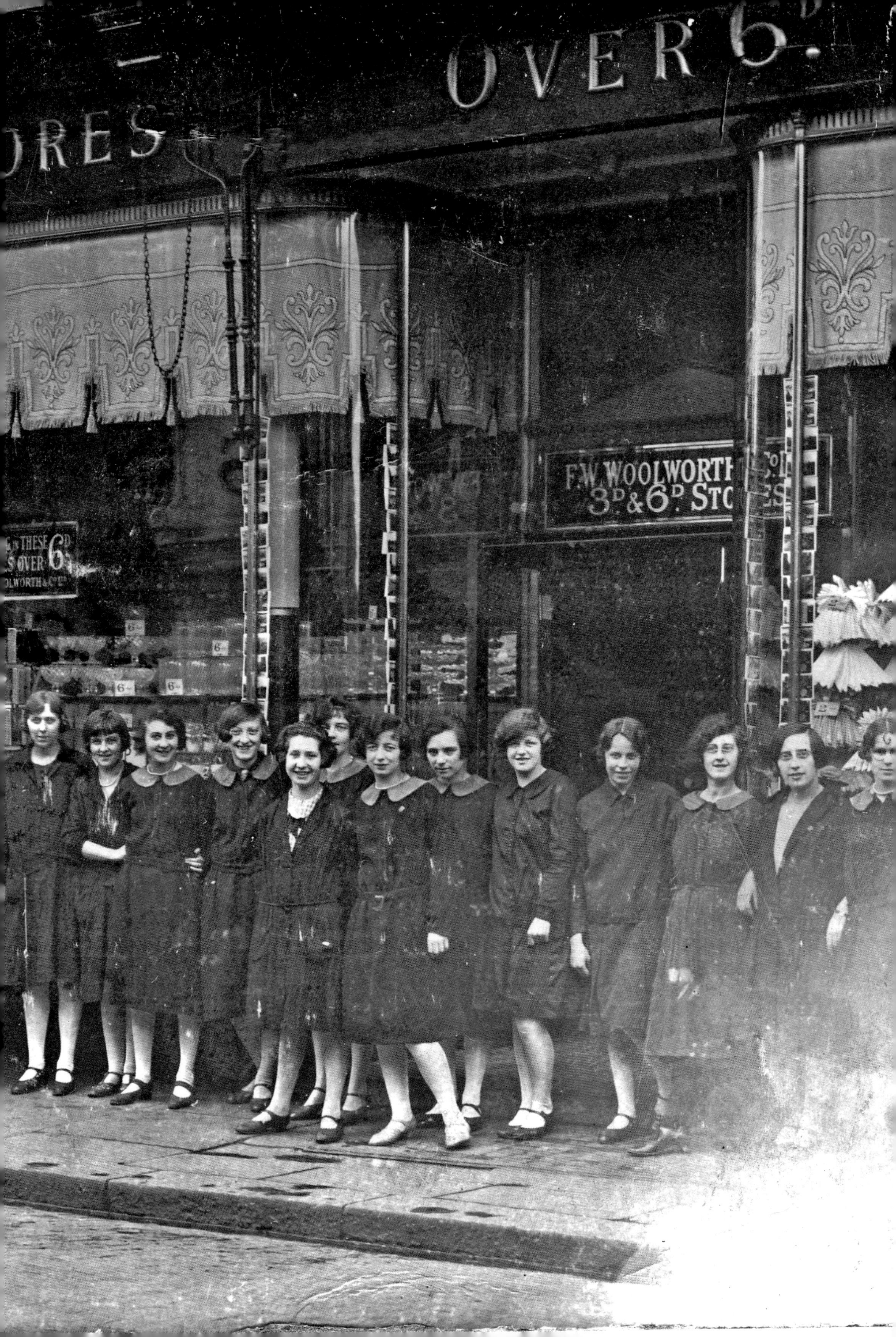

OVER 6D.
ORES
F.W. WOOLWORTH
3D & 6D STO

Firemen on picket duty at Swansea fire station, Grove Place during the 1976 firemen's strike.

Staff of the houseware department at David Evans' Princess Way store enter into the spirit of its French Week by dressing up, 1989.

Model vehicle assembly operatives at the Corgi factory, Fforestfach Industrial Estate, mid-1970s.

Engineers take a break during the switchover to a new telephone system in the telecommunications room of Singleton Hospital, 1991.

Staff at the Lottery kiosk run jointly by Glamorgan County Cricket Club and Swansea City AFC at the Oxford Street entrance to Swansea Market, serve another customer, early 1980s.

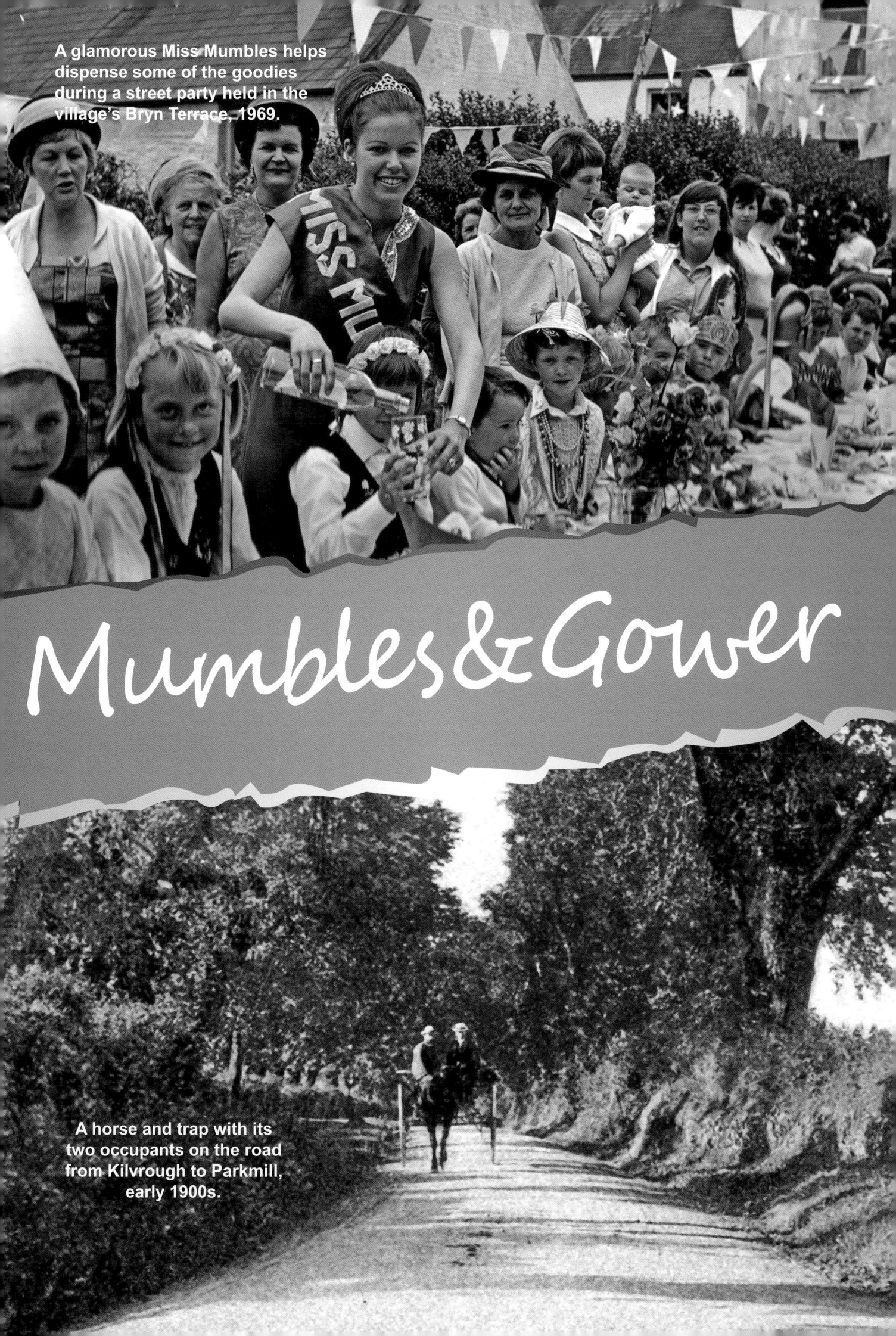

A glamorous Miss Mumbles helps dispense some of the goodies during a street party held in the village's Bryn Terrace, 1969.

Mumbles & Gower

A horse and trap with its two occupants on the road from Kilvrough to Parkmill, early 1900s.

The Rotherslade hotel, Langland, complete with tennis courts, 1903.

A tranquil village scene at Parkmill, Gower, 1920.

A van makes a delivery to a cottage at the bottom of the hill in Cheriton Village, 1930.

SWANSEA – THIS WAS YOUR LIFE!

Crowds stroll along the new road at Limeslade Bay, Mumbles, early 1900s.

Looking across Swansea Bay over the rooftops of Norton, Mumbles, 1920s.

Mumbles lighthouse and Bracelet Bay, 1952

The children's crazy golf course, Southend, July 1967.

SWANSEA – THIS WAS YOUR LIFE!

Caravan and camping sites at Horton and Porteynon, 1968.

Ponies on moorland at Ryers Down, Gower, July 1974.

Llanmadoc Church and graveyard, Gower, April 1968.

Part of Cheriton village, Gower, with fields, the marsh and Loughor Estuary behind, August 1970.

Three Cliffs, Bay, Gower, 1937.

A regimented row of beach huts at Langland Bay, February 1982. Behind them is Langland Bay Convalescent Home.

Construction work underway at Knab Rock, Southend, July 25, 1983.

Mumbles Pier and lifeboat station, 1975.

Verdi's Ice cream parlour, Knab Rock, 1996.

The Big Apple at Bracelet Bay
Mumbles, July 14, 2007.

SWANSEA – THIS WAS YOUR LIFE!

Dinghy enthusiasts put out to sea at Mumbles, against a backdrop of countless other craft at their moorings, August 1967.

Spectators crane their necks as they watch a cycle race at St Helen's sports ground, 1903.

Sports view

Skydivers all set to take off for another high flying adventure from Swansea Airport, late 1980s.

Glanmor Girls School netball team, 1925.

A bowling match underway at Brynmill Park, 1920s.

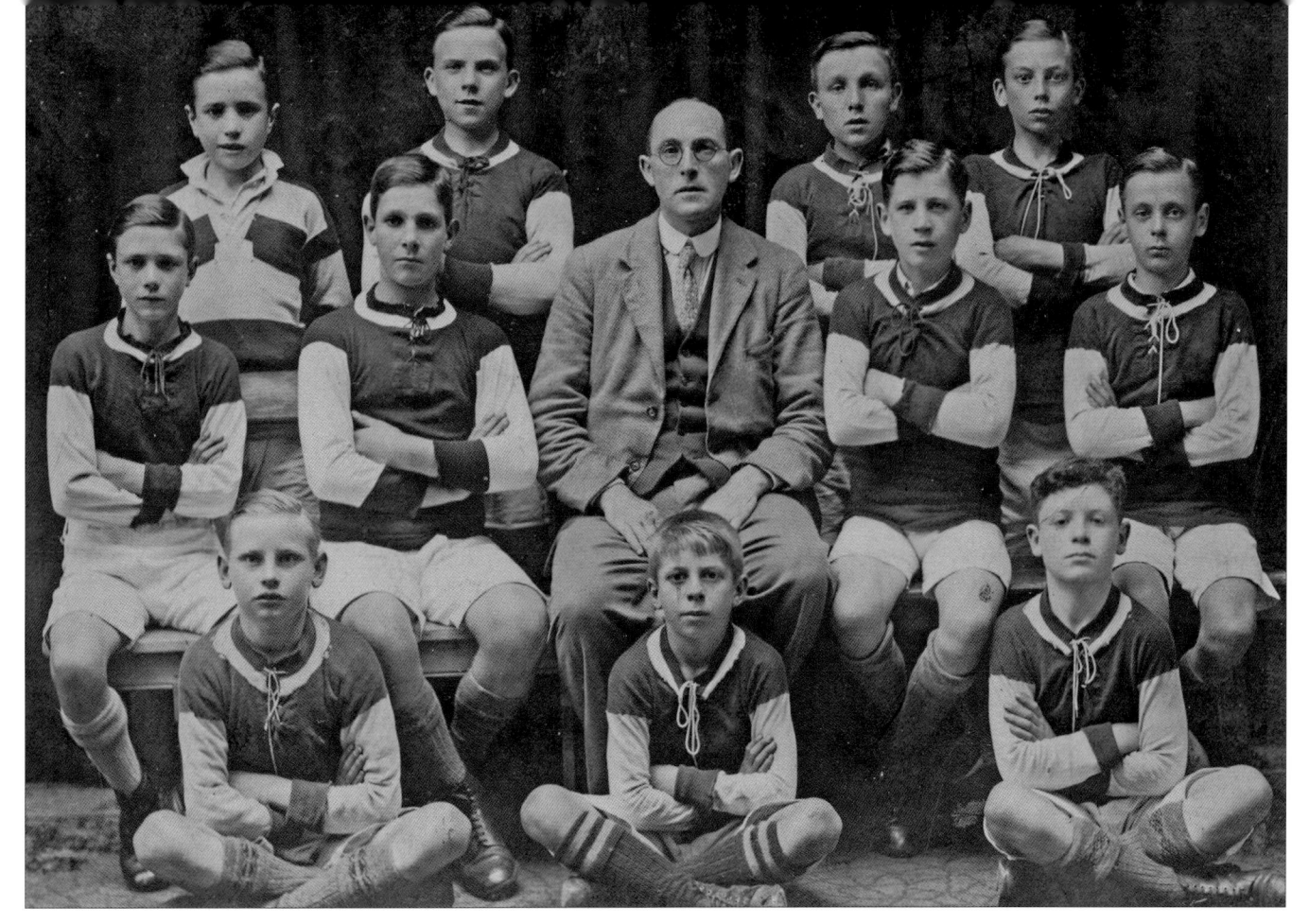

The football team at St Helen's Boys' School with their teacher in 1928-29, the season in which they were finalists in the Swansea Hospitals' Cup.

The rugby team of Dynevor School, 1934-35.

SWANSEA – THIS WAS YOUR LIFE!

Swansea Schoolboys football team, with officials and supporters prior to a match against Aston Boys, Birmingham, 1942.

Swansea Building Apprentices football team, 1946-47 season.

Miss Cissie Davies of Gwynedd-Avenue, Townhill, is presented by neighbours with a travelling bag before leaving for Norway to take part in a gymnastic festival, 1948. Mrs L Rees is seen handing over the gift.

Swansea Senior League Division Two champions Brunswick AFC, at Dublin on their Easter Tour of Ireland, 1949.

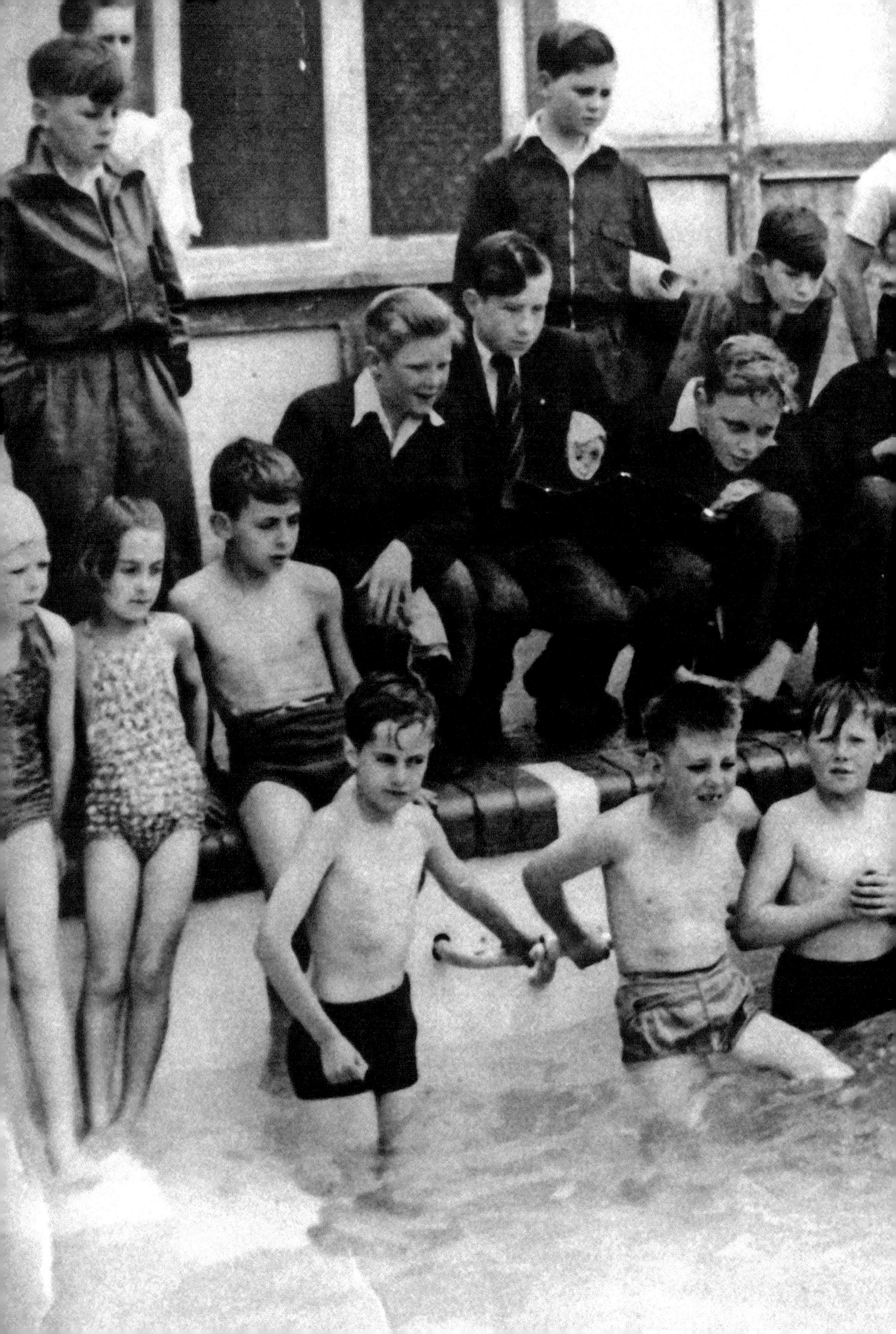

Swimming trainer Doc Morgan coaching youngsters at Morriston open air pool, 1953.

A Dynevor Grammar School, cricket X1, 1950 with teachers and headteacher.

A Bishop Gore School rugby team with teachers, 1953.

This was a special day for the pupils of Oxford Street Boys' School. They received a visit from Swansea Town players Reg Weston, and Roy Paul. Also with them is Swansea chairman Abe Freeman. Headmaster Pop Logan can be seen looking on, 1950.

Members of the Bishop Gore School's Under-15 cricket squad with teachers, 1952.

Bishop Gore Grammar School Rugby team with teacher Vivian Davies, the Father of Dr Who writer Russell T Davies, early 1950s.

A Richard Thomas & Baldwins works cricket team, 1950s.

SPORTS VIEW

Cockett Boys Club football team, mid-1950s.

A Port Tennant Stars football team, early 1960s.

SWANSEA – THIS WAS YOUR LIFE!

One of the junior rugby teams fielded by Bishop Gore School, 1952.

The cricket team of the Station Inn, St Thomas who were Eastside Cricket League Champions, complete with the trophy to prove it, mid-1950s.

Cockett Boys Club football team, 1955.

St Helen's Primary School rugby team, 1957. They went through the season unbeaten and did the double by beating Terrace Road School in the cup final as well as winning the league trophy.

SWANSEA – THIS WAS YOUR LIFE!

Swansea swimming trainer Doc Morgan with Glenda Phillips, who became a British and Olympic swimming champion; Michael Jones and Jim Ledger, late 1950s. The Doc Morgan Swimming Club became the Swansea Otters Swimming Club.

The cricket team of Martin Street School, Morriston, on a visit to Ascot where they played a team from Sunningdale School, 1959.

A school sports day at
Morfa Athletics Stadium,
Landore, June 1987.

Hafod School's senior football section A team 1958-59 which won the Swansea School's League Cup. Headmaster Ivor Simms is in the centre flanked by two teachers.

City of Swansea Swimming Club members and officials at St Helen's Road baths, mid-1970s.

Senior members and officers of Swansea Otters Swimming Club display some of the trophies won by members during a successful year's competition in the early 1960s.

A member of the Armine Club, Fforestfach, toasts his success in the Nolte Doubles Snooker Championship, 1967.

Members of the City of Swansea Swimming Club outside the Guildhall before embarking on a week-long tour of Jersey, 1978.

SWANSEA – THIS WAS YOUR LIFE!

Members of Olchfa Comprehensive School's under 18s netball team who were runners up in the West Glamorgan senior tournament held at the Afan Lido, Port Talbot, February 25, 1989. With the teacher in charge, Beverley Ann Jones, and head teacher John Booth.

Bowls enthusiast William Minty in action at Victoria Park, 1985.

SPORTS VIEW

Members of the BT's Swansea Golf Society on a visit to a Shrewsbury club, mid-1990s.

Members of Swansea City Retired Men's Bowls Club, 1979.

Visit www.bryngoldbooks.com for other titles available including:

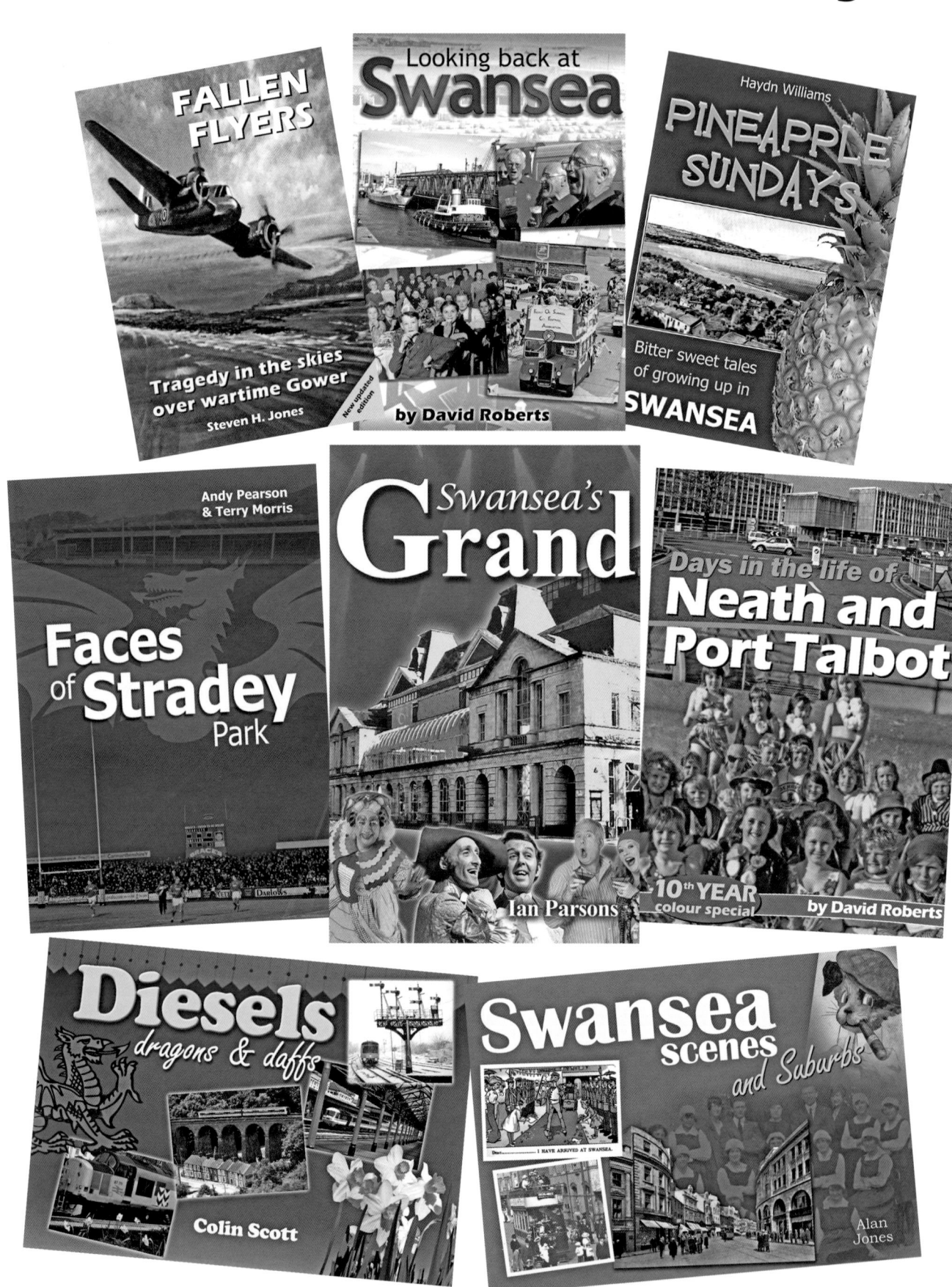

- **Fallen Flyers** — Tragedy in the skies over wartime Gower, Steven H. Jones
- **Looking back at Swansea** by David Roberts
- **Pineapple Sundays** — Bitter sweet tales of growing up in Swansea, Haydn Williams
- **Faces of Stradey Park**, Andy Pearson & Terry Morris
- **Swansea's Grand**, Ian Parsons
- **Days in the life of Neath and Port Talbot** — 10th YEAR colour special, by David Roberts
- **Diesels, dragons & daffs**, Colin Scott
- **Swansea scenes and Suburbs**, Alan Jones

To buy any of these titles tel: 01639 643961 or
email: info@bryngoldbooks.com
www.bryngoldbooks.com